THE EQUALITY MYTH

'. . . while the new female power can feel like an unstoppable force,
we cannot count on its momentum.
Forward motion is up to us.'

Naomi Wolf

'It is probably true to say that the largest scope for change
still lies in men's attitude to women,
and in women's attitude to themselves.'

Vera (Mary) Brittain

'Gone are the days of women succeeding
by learning to play men's games.
Instead the time has come for men on the move
to learn to play women's games.'

Tom Peters

THE
EQUALITY
MYTH

**A guide for women who want to make
a difference in the world of business
and for men who are ready for change**

Kerry Chater & Roma Gaster

ALLEN & UNWIN

First published in 1995 by
Allen & Unwin Pty Ltd
9 Atchison Street, St Leonards, NSW 2065 Australia

National Library of Australia
Cataloguing-in-Publication entry:

Chater, Kerry.
    The equality myth: a guide for women who want to make
    a difference in the world of business and for men who are
    ready for change.

    Bibliography.
    Includes index.
    ISBN 1 86373 830 4.

    1. Women in business. 2. Career development.
    3. Interpersonal communication. 4. Women executives.
    I. Gaster, Roma. II. Title.

650.1082

Set in 11.5/12.5 pt Adobe Garamond by DOCUPRO, Sydney
Printed by Southwood Press Pty Ltd, Sydney

10 9 8 7 6 5 4 3 2 1

This book is dedicated to all women and men who are searching for a better, more fulfilling way of living, being and working.

CONTENTS

ACKNOWLEDGMENTS

A wealth of people—family, friends, colleagues, publisher, editor, business associates—have made this book possible through their love, support, stories and feedback. The ideas we gained from talking with countless people have broadened our horizons and enriched the writing process. To these people we will be forever grateful.

Of no less value were the insights from the work of researchers, authors and pioneers, many of whom we have not met.

A number of women and men agreed to be interviewed and gave us permission to quote from them and to use their stories. We thank you for your time and your interest in changing the 'game' of business.

We have consciously chosen not to list the names of the people who have contributed to *The Equality Myth*, as we felt that the risk of unknowingly omitting someone was too great. We will be acknowledging and thanking each one of you in person.

Finally, we welcome any ideas and feedback that can enhance our efforts to make the world of business a more fulfilling place for both women and men.

ABOUT THE
AUTHORS

Roma Gaster was born of English and Irish parents and raised in Kenya, where she developed a love of nature and the animal world. She swam internationally for her country and was the champion swimmer and diver for Kenya until her family left for England, and then Australia, when she was 15.

Roma graduated from the University of Sydney with a Bachelor of Arts majoring in Economics and Japanese.

She has had over 15 years corporate experience in the areas of sales, research, advertising, marketing, management and training in the media, information technology, services and education industries. Over the last eight years, she has been involved in promoting and facilitating leading edge business and training methodologies in Australia and travels overseas continuously to research global trends and perspectives on business and education.

Roma is a co-founder of the education and training company Heart of Business, which is dedicated to training, consulting, researching and writing on a new philosophy of business embracing global interdependence, recognising and valuing gender and cultural diversity, new directions in leadership and empowering women and men to realise their potential.

She has co-developed and leads workshops for the corporate world based around the concepts of *The Equality Myth*.

Kerry Chater was born and grew up in Sydney. Her family constantly encouraged her to develop her thinking skills and a wide variety of interests, which include music, sport, creative writing and reading. She has two sons in their twenties, who are supportive and enthusiastic about the direction her career and her writing is taking.

Kerry has a Bachelor of Economics (Hons) degree, and a Masters degree in Educational Administration. Her work experience ranges from human resources management, administration, selling in the real estate and insurance industries, to teaching in both secondary and tertiary education and training in the corporate sector. For the last 10 years she has been involved in the provision of education and training courses in Australia, New Zealand and Asia.

She has a passion around helping people to realise their potential. Her attention right now is focused on women as she believes that for sustainable life to continue on Earth, women must play a more active role in leadership and decision making at the corporate level, at government level, and at world level.

INTRODUCTION

For so long, women have been striving to achieve equality. Yet what do we mean by equality? Do we mean being the same as men? Do we mean being treated the same as men, or having the same rights as men?

This issue did not interest us until the early 1990s when we were asked to write a workbook and trainers' guide for a video on the glass ceiling. At the end of the process we were full of questions. Why in practise are women in business having so much difficulty breaking through the barrier that has become known as the 'glass ceiling'? Is it because men are shutting us out? If so, why are they shutting us out? And the questions that really started to interest us were:

- Are women the same as men, or are we different?

- Is equality the right goal to go for?

- Will more women in positions of power and influence mean more of the same, or will it inevitably lead to changes in the way we do things?

- As more women become involved in the management and leadership of businesses, will the world of business contain more heart, compassion and nurturing?

These sound like feminist issues, although until now we have not consciously considered ourselves to be feminists, or been involved in the nuances of feminist thought and activism. And yet, we have come to realise, we are both feminists in the sense articulated by Naomi Wolf in *Fire with Fire* (1993). She says that being a feminist means 'I am a sentient, strong individual who objects to being held back—or having other women held back—on the basis of gender' (p. 151). And feminism . . . 'is at heart the logical extension of democracy . . .' (p. 336).

At the same time, our interests extend beyond women to the global economy, to the changes that are occurring in organisational structures and values, and to a deep concern with the environmental damage our existing system is causing. It seems to us that there has to be a better way of doing things, a way that is effective while respecting and valuing other people, other cultures and the environment.

Our experience, our research and our discussions with countless women and men—business owners, managers and executives all over the world—has convinced us that this better way is within our grasp if we can utilise the power of one single, undervalued resource—**women!**

The evidence is that women and men are different, and these differences go much deeper than the obvious physical and biological differences. We have different ways of thinking, of communicating, of making decisions, of taking risks, of working and managing. And yet the 'male' way of doing things predominates. Women make up 52 per cent of the world's population but we are treated as a minority, and our approaches and the roles we are allocated by the existing system tend to be undervalued. We have colluded in this process by acting as a minority, and silently accepting the roles and values imposed on us.

This led us to ask even more questions. We live in and accept without question a world that has been set up by men according to patriarchal values. Why do we do this? Is this way of operating really giving us the outcomes that we want? Is there a better way? Why have women remained so disenfranchised for so long? Why doesn't the male culture want to include us?

In this book we question our blind acceptance of the patriarchy and the limits it has been imposing on women for thousands of years. Through the advances made by feminism and the opportunities given to us by rapid technological change, we have today a unique opportunity for asserting our power and our ability to make a difference. And it could well be that, once we embrace and value differences, we may find that men, just as much as women, have the capacity to include caring and heart in business.

We accept the notion of diversity when we talk about different cultures. Yet why do we strive for equality or 'sameness' between the genders? Women and men are *not* the same, and we feel that our very differences offer us the chance to redress some of the negative effects of the patriarchy. In fact, a true partnership between women and men offers us the best hope that humankind has for the future.

But in order to reach our potential and play highly visible and influential roles in business and in the global economy, women need real 'how to' strategies. This book offers those strategies. We have synthesised and drawn on the work of many researchers, corporate trainers and authors. In doing so we have depended on certain models which we have used in our own lives in order to gain a deeper personal understanding of ourselves and of others.

The exercises, stories and quotations have been chosen to assist you in assimilating and internalising the information so that you can use it in your daily life, both in business and personally. We hope that new possibilities will open up for you as a result of reading our thoughts and experiences.

The models and diagrams used are intended to stimulate possibilities for change and to expand choices, not to categorise people into certain 'behaviour boxes'. They will have achieved their purpose if they offer you finer distinctions and more behavioural choices and flexibility.

The Equality Myth is for all women and men who want to understand, empower and enrich each other so that the future for all humankind can be brighter.

1

LIVING IN A PATRIARCHY . . .

'There's an old Chinese proverb:

Women Hold Up Half The Sky

It means that half the work and half the thinking in the world
is done by women.
For the sky to be complete,
both halves must work together;
nothing can be truly human that excludes one half of humanity.'

Sally Helgesen[1]

. . . HOW IT IS FOR WOMEN

We have been living in a patriarchy—a male-dominated culture—for
so long that we have no experience or memory of things being any
other way. We tend to take the system in which we live for granted,
without questioning the values on which it is based, and the effects
it has on the non-male half of humanity—women.

Put simply, living in a patriarchy means that our way of life has
been set up according to male values. The key leadership and power
positions tend to be predominantly in the hands of males. The
system is based on power, strength and control, and tends to value
material progress, profit and wealth and to foster aggression, competition, winners and losers, haves and have nots.

Over the centuries, women have been placed in an under-class
position. Until recently, in most Western cultures, women could
not own property, inherit, do business on their own, vote, or even
claim control over their own bodies. They have been made to feel
inferior and subservient to males. While male tasks, sports and
interests have been highly valued, traditional female tasks (child-
bearing, caring for the family, maintaining the home, providing food
and clothes) have been taken for granted and undervalued. This

discrimination still exists in so-called developed countries, and is even stronger in developing countries. In a 1993 UNICEF diary it is claimed that:

> Women are the main cultivators of land and the major producers of food in developing countries, especially in Africa. They also prepare the food for their entire families.
>
> But in many countries, women face severe discrimination. Even as babies, the girl child is weaned earlier than the boy child. Girls often are served last at mealtime, and receive less parental attention, education, medical care, and job training than boys do.[2]

Patriarchal values are alive and well!

In the patriarchal system the male is seen to have greater value than the female. The education of sons is more important than that of daughters, as the role for which the daughter is being groomed is that of wife and mother; men are leaders and executives while women are assistants, secretaries and clerks. The person being groomed for the CEO position is a man; family businesses are handed on to sons.

Ivor, who migrated from Yugoslavia some 40 years ago, has built up a sawmill business north of Sydney. His elder son was installed as the managing director of the business in 1990 while Ivor and his wife took six months' holiday (their first for twenty years!) in Yugoslavia. In that six months, the son managed to run a thriving business into the ground. On his parents' return, he was sent to a subsidiary in Queensland. He proceeded to mismanage and financially cripple this business as well before Ivor finally fired him.

The younger son runs a machine shop in the sawmill. He is in charge of $500 000 worth of equipment which is left lying around, new parts are indistinguishable from broken parts, there is a dangerous amount of oil and grease on the shop floor, food remains are scattered everywhere, safety standards are disregarded, and the staff are demotivated.

The daughter also works in the business. While she clearly enjoys her work, Ivor is apologetic that she has to work. She is their sales representative and is on the road three weeks out of four. She and the father (who has invented some of the equipment they use in the sawmill and who manages the processing of the timber) are the dynamic and effective parts of the business.

Shares in the business are divided between the father and the two sons. In other words, the mother and the daughter have no share. Despite the incompetence of the sons, they will inherit the business.

The patriarchal system could not have survived for all of these centuries without the cooperation of ordinary people. Women, just as much as men, have internalised the rules.

Both women and men maintain and pass on the stereotypes, and thus the system—the female images of low self-esteem, low status, inability to do certain jobs, weakness, the need for male protection, and so on. Even today we hear women being put down when a mother says to her young son, 'You run like a girl,' or a father berates his teenage son with 'Long hair is sissy'.

And women unconsciously support the patriarchy by continuing to do most of the world's unpaid work, by caring for and sustaining their families physically, emotionally and economically, by making things work, no matter how much they are oppressed and abused, and by putting the needs of their spouse and family before their own needs.

Jessie's story . . .

I always wanted to go into business, and yet there always seemed to be a good reason not to.

I remember the Depression of the 1930s well. My father went off looking for work wherever he could get it, while my mother kept the family together and ran our butcher's shop. I can still see her lifting and cutting up carcasses all by herself. I had to leave school and get a job when I was 14, just so we could make ends meet.

I was 20 when I married George, and my mother told me how lucky I was. He was a good man, who didn't drink, smoke, womanise or gamble. And he *has* been a good husband. He was brought up to believe that men should provide for and protect their families.

George went into business with his father. I wanted to help, so I was allowed to work in the office for a while, and I went with George on business trips. But I was never permitted to become part of the business. George's father didn't approve of working wives.

After our first child was at school, I decided to go into business for myself. I had a real passion for cooking exotic cakes and desserts, and felt that I could successfully open a cake shop. My father-in-law actively discouraged my idea, and George talked me into having another child. Six years later the same thing happened. And then, somehow, the opportunity to go into business for myself was lost. George's business was doing very well, and between travelling, entertaining and looking after the children, there was no time for my dreams.

George and I are in our seventies now, and our children all have their own children. Looking back, looking after George and the children has not been enough for me. I feel unfulfilled. I would still like to know if I could have made it in business. I should have been stronger, but at the time it all seemed too hard and I didn't want to upset George. The most positive thing I have done is to make sure my daughters had a good education and to help them to be independent and self-sufficient.

THE BEGINNINGS OF CHANGE

Not all women accept the rules. Gradually more and more women are becoming dissatisfied with the way things are. We have begun the long, slow, frustrating process of claiming our rights. Until now, the struggle has been to be treated the same as men, to achieve equality.

So we have fought for the right to education, the right to vote, the right to control our own bodies, the right to equal pay for equal work.

In the 1970s there was a wave of feminism that caused a revolution in how women see themselves. As a result, women are strongly entrenched in the workforce, and working wives and mothers are now the norm and not the exception. The behaviour and expectations of Western women in the 1990s are fundamentally different from that of our mothers and grandmothers.

This is a huge leap forward, and yet we still haven't achieved 'equality' with men.

For example, while women have been allowed into the paid workforce, we have largely been kept at the lower status levels of organisations, paid less than men and perceived as having a lesser value than men. The perception is still that our main role is in the unpaid workforce as wives and mothers. In the words of Carolyn Brand, in 1993 the highest ranking female officer in the Royal Australian Navy:

> Men have let women into the fringes—the areas that don't really matter—but protect the centre, the really plum areas. They protect the system because they really believe that women can't do the jobs. Everything in their experience and their background tells them women can't do the jobs.[3]

Women today . . .

are
52% of the world's population

do
66% of the world's work

receive
less than 10% of wages and salaries

own
less than 1% of the world's wealth

represent only
1% of the world's leadership[4]

Despite the achievements that have been made, this is still stark inequality, a gross imbalance of power. And the future picture is no brighter. The International Labour Office of the United Nations has estimated that if women continue to progress at the current rate, it will take 500 years before we have equal managerial status with men and a further 475 years before we hold equal political and economic status.[5]

Why are we making such slow progress? Is it because we have been striving for the wrong goal? Anne Summers seems to have put her finger on it in her 1975 book *Damned Whores and God's Police*, when she said: 'To demand equality is to concede that the standards and practices devised by and for men are the most desirable . . .'.[6] More recently, Naomi Wolf has suggested that the goal of equality may be limiting us. After all, as she says, we are a majority of the world's population and are entitled to 'true democracy in which the advantage of our numbers makes us the single strongest force on earth'.[7]

What we have been doing, unconsciously, is accepting that the patriarchal system in which we have grown up is the only way of doing things. And yet this system undervalues women. Where differences between women and men are acknowledged, the contributions of women are not seen as having equal worth. How can there ever be equality, let alone true democracy, for women on a male playing field? All the rules are loaded against us.

We must take off our blinkers and look long and hard at the patriarchal system. What has it achieved? Whom does it benefit? Whom does it disadvantage? What are its negative effects?

> *WE BELIEVE THAT WOMEN AND MEN*
> *ARE CREATED DIFFERENT . . .*
>
> *THE DIFFERENCES ARE COMPLEMENTARY . . .*
>
> *IT'S TIME TO VALUE THE DIFFERENCES*

On the positive side, the patriarchal system has given us many benefits. In this century alone, rapid progress has meant that many of us in the Western world are able to live longer and enjoy more comfortable and healthy lifestyles. Few of us would choose to go back to a subsistence way of living.

And yet there have always been costs. The lack of power, undervaluing and sometimes oppression of women has been an ongoing cost through the centuries. We are now becoming aware of even more negative effects. The obsession with power, control and progress for their own sakes is taking its toll on the environment. The imbalances between developed and less developed countries are becoming greater. There is rampant pollution, static or declining living standards in the majority of the world's economies, and localised wars and unrest on an unprecedented scale in living memory. Famine and devastation caused by natural disasters are endemic. If we continue on our current path it is likely that the world will soon become a nightmare environment of deserts, eroded mountains, dead coral reefs and barren oceans, suitable only for the hardiest and most adaptable of species such as cockroaches, rats and weeds.[8]

Since the beginnings of patriarchy, we have moved from:

- **a nomadic to an agrarian system**
  This era lasted for about six thousand years and is epitomised by the feudal structure, where the male was the dominant figure, the aggressor and the competitor, and his contribution was seen as being much more valuable than the female's.

- **an agrarian to an industrial system**
  This era lasted for around two hundred years and was characterised by the factories that developed as a result of the discovery of steam power and other inventions, and that depended on an unskilled and powerless workforce. The male maintained superiority by imposing a new male-dominated game of work cultures, rules and structures, and by controlling information.

- **an industrial base to a system of rapidly changing technology**
  Here information is readily available and is the key to personal power and success. This era is with us today in developed economies and is likely to continue at an accelerating pace in the twenty-first century.

The needs of the information age are inconsistent with the structures, bureaucracies and rules of the industrial era. In the global economy that we have today, aggressive competition and win/lose strategies are working less and less effectively.

Ironically in some ways, we are now witnessing changes in business values and structures. It is ironic because the product of the system—technological advancement—is forcing change on the system that created it! At the same time, women are, for the first time, a significant proportion of the workforce. While the industrial society was created by men for men, the information society and beyond needs people, both male and female, who are well educated and technically trained. This has created a unique opportunity for women as all levels of the business hierarchy are now potentially open to us.

Backlash

Yet the movement of women into influential positions is not happening smoothly. There is a lot of talk at present about a backlash—a revitalised and sometimes violent reaction against women in non-traditional roles. For example, Susan Faludi, Marilyn French and Naomi Wolf[9] have all written recently about observed backlashes against women. While this backlash argument has met with the full gamut of reactions—from hostile condemnation to agreement—what we know about the patriarchy makes backlashes against women inevitable. Whether they realise they are doing it or not, men in positions of power are fighting to retain the system they have created and which has worked so well for them.

The world of business as we know it today is predominantly controlled by males who are over 50, conservative and reluctant to change. Even some of the men who are under 50 feel threatened by any kind of change. Unconsciously then, these men are engaged in a rearguard action to defend what they know and put off the unknown and unfamiliar (and inevitable) for as long as possible.

Sometimes the struggle is overt, as in the moves in the United States to make abortion a criminal offence or attempts in the churches to oppose the ordination of women. But feminism and antidiscrimination laws have had their effect, and today the backlash is mostly subtle. For example:

- a 'knowingness' that a man will make the best senior executive for the organisation

- attention being focused in meetings on the contributions by men

- mother-in-law and wife jokes

- women's abilities and preferences in certain areas being put down—such as driving a car, reading a map, showing emotion

- degrading remarks about values such as caring, compassion, understanding.

THE 'GAME'

In the Western business world, we see the backlash in relation to the 'game' of business. The rules of the 'game' are not spelt out in any business school curriculum, but they are nevertheless deeply entrenched and blindly obeyed.

The 'game' is about hierarchy, power, control, domination and competition—where there is a winner and a loser. But if we are going to understand it better, and in particular understand why women have difficulty in playing the 'game' successfully, we need to think differently, think outside the box. One way of doing this is to ask ourselves what the 'game' isn't.

We have borrowed a definition[10] which goes:

> *A game . . .*
>
> **WHERE WHAT**
> **ISN'T**
> **IS MORE**
> **IMPORTANT**
> **THAN WHAT**
> **IS**

So, if we know what the 'game' is, the question then becomes, what isn't it?

What it *isn't* is:

role sharing	*responsibility*	*caring*	*creative*
interdependence	*accountability*	*compassion*	*global*
life sustaining	*long term*	*inclusive*	*diverse*

And yet it has been possible for some men, such as artists, poets and philosophers, to play successfully in the area of what the 'game' isn't. So the missing ingredient about what the 'game' isn't, is that it is not female. The 'game' of business is a male game.

This helps to explain why women have found it so difficult to move into levels of power and influence. In general, the women who have succeeded—for example, Indira Gandhi, Margaret Thatcher and Martina Navratilova—have been adept at playing the male game.

But what is happening now is that the playing field of the 'game' is changing. We are moving from industrialisation where the patriarchal model worked so brilliantly to an era where our survival and progress will depend, not on our ability to set rules, control production lines, establish bureaucracies, assert status and focus on the bottom line, but on our ability to communicate, negotiate, work with emotions, create new solutions to ever-changing problems and opportunities, respond to change, think globally and strategically and work with and value people.

None of us—neither women nor men—can go on playing the old rules on the new playing field. It is our assertion that the playing field is moving in the direction of feminine values, so that what the 'game' now needs are the skills that women can bring to it.

And this is the process that is being delayed because of backlashes and resistance to change. The challenge is to find a path to speed up the natural evolution from the old to the new, from the existing to the future. We need a true valuing of difference in order to create a more sustainable future for both womankind and mankind.

> *'I predict the first country or culture*
> *which truly blends men's and women's*
> *strengths will be the next world power'.*
> Robert Kiyosaki[11]

A NEW PARADIGM

What we are looking at is a shift in the way we think about organisations, about leadership, and, in particular, in the way we look at women and our role in the business world and in the global economy. And it is because a shift is required that it is so difficult for those entrenched in the system to see it and to understand what is happening. The reasons are put succinctly by Joel A. Barker in his book, *Discovering the Future*:[12]

- How we see the world is strongly influenced by our existing paradigms or 'set of rules'.

- Present paradigms are comfortable for us; we are used to operating within them, and so we resist changing them.

- It is usually someone from outside the system who creates the new paradigm.

- When a paradigm shift occurs, the practitioners of the old paradigm lose much or all of their leverage.

Both women and men are affected by a paradigm shift in the way we work and live, although clearly men have a greater vested interest in the old, existing paradigm. But change is occurring, despite all the forces of resistance. The acceleration in new technology is forcing it on us. And yet it is not enough to wait for it to happen, and to trust that, naturally and inevitably, women will be significant players in the new paradigm.

We need to take action. The question is, what sort of action should we take? How can we ensure that the contributions of women and men are valued equally and seen as complementary?

TAKING THE FIRST STEP

To begin with we must look at ourselves. We must look at our own values and beliefs. Are we happy with the existing situation? Do we want to change the way it is, the way in which women are valued, the power base held by women? Are we happy to continue to strive for the goal of equality? Are we prepared to value the difference between women and men? Are we prepared to change ourselves, and to become more flexible? And if we want to change, what is it that we have to *be, do* and *have* in order to produce these changes?

Once we understand the limitations that the patriarchy has imposed on women, we are in a position to make a difference. And once we have decided that change is desirable, then the only thing that can hold women back is themselves!

This might sound like a strongly judgmental statement, yet it is intended to be supportive! Claiming that women are the only ones who can hold themselves back means, by definition, that no one else can hold any power over us. So often we see people becoming victims because they give their power away to someone else. When you give someone else the power to choose what is or isn't appropriate for you, you take away your own ability to make choices for yourself. It is only when you accept responsibility for your own life that you have the ability to choose your own path and accept the consequences of the choices you make.

As teenagers we fight to assert our independence from our parents. Yet why is it that so many women give away their power to their spouses, their in-laws, sometimes even their children?

Take another example. John Naisbitt and Patricia Aburdene say, 'To reach top positions around the year 2000 women in their late thirties and forties must begin *now* to think like the CEOs they never planned or dreamed they could be'.[13] But many women seem to believe that leadership is a male domain. This is a huge self-imposed (and probably unconscious) limitation. And as long as it continues, what are the chances of significant numbers of women moving into influential positions?

The question is, how do we change old habits, old behaviours, old ways of accepting the system as it is?

The answer lies within. In order to change what is not working, we first need to bring it to conscious awareness. What won't work for women in a new system that values difference is continued dependence on men. We need to question our way of communicating, whom we choose as role models, how we make decisions, our ability to take risks and the lack of opportunity for women to become highly visible.

Once we have asked these questions, we need to look at our own internal motivators—what drives us. This involves understanding factors that have probably been largely unconscious in most of us, factors such as our attitudes, beliefs and values . . .

2

FOR THINGS TO CHANGE . . .

'Those who know others are intelligent;
Those who know themselves have insight.
Those who master others have force;
Those who master themselves have strength.'

Lao Tsu[1]

. . . FIRST I MUST CHANGE

Where does the belief that change is possible and the willingness to change begin?

It begins with conscious awareness. Most of us are not aware of the factors determining our behaviour. In order to change, it is important to get to know what makes us tick—what makes us happy, or sad, or motivated, or angry.

It is particularly in the areas of values, beliefs and attitudes that women have been disadvantaged by the patriarchy. So, over the next two chapters, we will look in detail at these factors. The purpose is to bring values, beliefs and attitudes to conscious awareness and to demonstrate how it is possible for us to change any of them.

VALUES

We will use the analogy of a tree to show the factors that determine our behaviours. The deepest layers of behaviour (for example, factors that determine personality) are shown as the tree trunk: thick, stable, substantial, firmly rooted in the ground and relatively inflexible.

Values form the major branches of the tree: solid but more flexible than the trunk, reaching out in all directions and a key component of the tree's structure and growth (see figure 2.1).

Figure 2.1

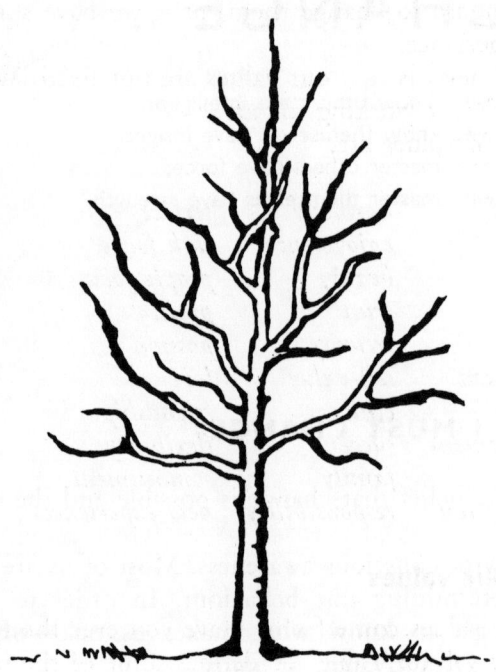

Values provide the driving force behind all our actions. They are the rules we have for ourselves. They give us our motivation and purpose in life. It is through our values that we judge appropriateness and inappropriateness, right and wrong, good and bad.

Unconsciously we rank our values in order of importance to us, and we satisfy our values according to this ranking. So if, for example, 'power' is the most important value to us, we will unconsciously strive to satisfy our need for 'power' before any other value.

It is possible to acquire and change values at any stage of our lives, and there are many differing views on how this happens.[2] Some claim that our values evolve over our lives in seven-year cycles. Morris Massey, a sociologist, says that we go through three distinct periods of values and personality development.[3] The three major periods correspond to the ages between birth and 7, from around 8 to 13 and from 14 to 21. While our values continue to evolve over time and with age, our strongest values will only change if we consciously choose to change them, or if we have some significant emotional experience.

The good news is . . . our values are not fixed. We can change them if they're not working for us.

Examples of values are:

work ethic	*harmony*	*service*	*satisfaction*
power	*enjoyment*	*task focus*	*achievement*
privacy	*beauty*	*people focus*	*honesty*
respect	*trust*	*profit*	*integrity*
status	*security*	*passion*	*loyalty*
empowerment	*self-value*	*love*	*freedom*
leadership	*ethics*	*friendship*	*wealth*
self-development	*success*	*flexibility*	*relationships*
health	*family*	*commitment*	*money*
communication	*responsibility*	*new experiences*	

Sources of our values

Where do our values come from? Have you ever thought about the source of your values? Table 2.1 defines some of the major sources.

Table 2.1   Source of values

Personal	System	Work
Family		
Friends		
School	Country	
Religion	Government	
Culture	The media	Company vision
Role models	War mentality	Management
Economic prosperity	Economic thought	Peer group
Historical events	Research	Line of work
Generational	Patriarchy/matriarchy	Industry
Archetypes	Leadership	Mentor
Genetics		
Gender		

Values are very personal and individual. Each of us has unique experiences and the main sources of our strongest values—family, friends, school, work and the culture and environment in which we grow up—affect each of us differently. We also tend to have different values at different stages of our lives.

As well, every generation has different values, based on significant experiences that occurred when they were growing up. For example, people who are in their forties in the 1990s—the baby boomers—were enormously influenced as a group by television, computers and the materialism of their early childhood years in the 1950s and early 1960s. In contrast, people who are in their sixties in the 1990s grew up during the disruption to family life and scarcity of goods experienced during World War II, and this has had a strong influence on their values as a group.[4]

Teenagers in the 1960s and 1970s who hero-worshipped music idols adopted the values and behaviours of the drug culture. It was considered to be 'cool' to do drugs because the bands were into drugs and wrote songs about drugs. This behaviour was also reinforced by the peer group. Today most world-famous musicians and singers realise their responsibility in influencing fans and are publicly stating their support for positive global changes. This in turn is shaping the values of thousands of their supporters.

Are female values different from male values?

Let's take a look at how we grow up . . .

As women, our values are shaped on a macro scale by a male-dominated political, economic and social system. The key figures of success, power and leadership for children are men. For boys there are an abundance of male role models both at the macro and micro levels. For girls, female role models mostly exist at the micro level—mothers, female relations and friends, school teachers and religious figures. In addition there are movie and pop stars, queens and princesses, female sporting figures and the occasional woman who 'makes it' in politics or business.

As a result, feminine values continue to emphasise supportive and nurturing roles. The following is a typical female hierarchy of values:

harmony	*enjoyment*	*family*	*responsibility*
service	*friendship*	*love*	*caring and nurturing*
loyalty	*commitment*	*receptivity*	*relationships*

A male hierarchy of values is likely to include:

power	*status*	*success*	*achievement*
money	*profit*	*wealth*	*task focus*
freedom	*control*	*security*	*independence*

Small wonder that men still hold the highly visible positions in business and politics in a culture that values competition, success, task focus and logical, linear thinking while women in business continue to struggle, and often give up and accept the status quo.

Knowing that this is how it has been up until now does not imply that we cannot do something to change it for the future. We have so much information available now on how our brains work and how we can in fact change and shape our lives.

> *'It is important to learn*
> *what your values are*
> *so you will be able to direct, motivate*
> *and support yourself*
> *at the deepest level.'*
> Anthony Robbins[5]

Knowing our own values can help us predict our responses and actions. This helps us to understand the results that keep turning up in our lives. It also helps us to understand the 'why' and the 'how' of our actions and behaviours.

The easiest way to understand values and how they work is to start with your own. We have included two simple exercises at the end of the book to show how easy it is to identify, rank and change your own values (see page 188).

What do you notice between your personal life values and your work values? Are they the same? The 'game' of business has its own set of values, and many women find that one of the hardest things to deal with in the corporate world is the conflict between personal values and corporate values born out of a male-dominated patriarchal system. Becoming consciously aware of a clash of values is a first step toward resolving the conflict.

Lynne's story . . .

Within two years of joining a large financial planning
organisation, Lynne had become general manager, Northern
Region. The organisation was established and controlled by
a self-made entrepreneur in his early forties, whose values
centred around family, inclusion, integrity, acknowledgment,
shared decision making, honesty, openness, empowerment,
communication and service.

He was made a takeover offer that was too good to
refuse. Within weeks the organisation started to change,
reflecting the different culture and values of the new parent
company. These values aligned with a typical male-dominated hierarchical organisation and included status, control,
top-down decision making, rigidity, authority and a profit-
centred mindset.

For Lynne, and many other previously loyal employees,
there was a major conflict of values. Lynne left the organisation soon after and has since set up her own company.

It is important to understand our own values, and the values we
are experiencing in organisations, so that we can make informed
decisions about the right path for us. If we choose to play the
business 'game,' we are then in a better position to develop strategies
which are going to help us both to remain consistent with our own
values and to achieve our career goals.

So, now that we understand individual values, let us look at
traditional corporate values and at some of the newer trends in
organisations.

CORPORATE VALUES

In the bigger corporate 'game', things are changing. Just as personal
values evolve through life, we are experiencing a gradual shift in the
values and philosophies of organisations.

The traditional organisation

The traditional organisation is a product of the Industrial Revolution. It has as its base the wisdom of economic thought and conventional management theory that values the profit motive and glorifies the virtues of rational, non-emotive, theory-based business practices, decision making and planning. The ultimate purpose of this business model is to make a profit at all costs. Employees are expendable resources to be controlled and manipulated. Natural resources are also regarded in the same way—as infinitely renewable.

In the traditional organisation, power comes from status and money. Values include:

competition	*status*	*bottom-line focus*
authority	*control*	*'old boys' network*
win/lose	*conformity*	*rules and regulations*
stability	*manipulation*	*'top down' decision making*
hierarchy	*lack of trust*	*divide and conquer*
conservatism	*short-term goals*	*respect for position*
rigidity	*political games*	*'tell' style leadership*
hard work ethic		

Until recently this way of operating was considered to be highly successful and efficient. But things are changing. Since the 1980s we have witnessed the ending of the Cold War, global environmental crises, economic and political turmoil, continuing internal and international conflicts, as well as accelerating waves of technological change. The magnitude of these issues has forced us, for the first time, to question the wisdom of our political and socio-economic structures.

Within organisations questions are also being asked about the efficiency, validity and ethics of traditional business practices. What is needed in the current climate of socio-economic uncertainty and rapid technological change are organisations that can respond quickly to changing conditions, that are flexible and can generate new ideas, new products and new strategies. The traditional organisation finds it difficult to do this because of its emphasis on hierarchy, authority structures, inflexible rules and procedures, and its inability to encourage creativity at all levels of the organisation.

The emerging organisation

The organisational form that is emerging has changed its focus from task and profits to include broader global concerns and people. Power comes from a shared vision and knowledge, and people are empowered to be innovative, to contribute and to lead by example. Teamwork, cooperation and flexibility are more important than supervision and control. While these changes are uncomfortable and threatening for individuals who like the security of rigid structures, hierarchies and set roles, it does allow organisations to respond quickly and creatively to changing conditions.

In the emerging organisation, power comes from shared knowledge and power. Values include:

win/win	*love*	*adding value*
cooperation	*compassion*	*social responsibility*
passion	*caring*	*'fun' work ethic*
earned respect	*ethics*	*open communication*
creativity	*trust*	*promotion on merit*
contribution	*self-esteem*	*open networks*
empowerment	*agreement*	*long-term focus*
flexibility	*service*	

Anita Roddick, in her book *Body and Soul*, talks about the contrasts between the values on which she has built her global business, The Body Shop, and traditional business values:

What we are trying to do is to create a new business paradigm, simply showing that business can have a human face and a social conscience . . . we are trying to . . . create a business environment in which people are happy and fulfilled, so that they feel good about what they are doing and good about themselves . . . I think all business practices would improve immeasurably if they were guided by 'feminine' principles—qualities like love and care and intuition . . .

The status quo says that the business of business is to make profits. We have always challenged that. For us the business of business is to keep the company alive and breathlessly excited, to protect the workforce, to be a force for good in our society and then, after all that, to think of the speculators . . .

As a result of what we have learned during the last fifteen years, we have evolved a simple credo. It goes like this: you can run a business differently from the way most businesses are run; you can share your prosperity with your employees and empower them without being in fear of them; you can rewrite the book in terms of how a company interacts with the community; you can rewrite the book on Third World trade and global responsibility and on the role of educating the company, customers and share-holders; finally, you can do all this and still play the game according to the City, still raise money, delight the institutions and give shareholders a wondrous return on their investment.[6]

The values and philosophies of the emerging organisation are more congruent with feminine values. And the Body Shop is an example of feminine values successfully applied in business. It serves as a beacon to the future—to a new way of running businesses that is profitable, that empowers employees, that is innovative and responsive to change, that is globally and environmentally aware, and that values female and male contributions equally.

Another example of the changes taking place is the 'shamrock' organisation identified by Charles Handy in *The Age of Unreason*.[7] Here, instead of the traditional monolithic structure, organisations are made up of three different parts (like the three leaves of a shamrock):

- a small core of full-time professionals, technicians and managers

- a fringe of self-employed professionals and technical specialists who are contracted by the organisation (for example, desktop publishers, cleaners, consultants, painters, computer program-mers)

- a flexible labour force of part-time, temporary workers who are used to meeting peaks in demand

As Charles Handy says, this form of organisation makes economic sense. But it also means that there are three different workforces rather than one, and each has to be managed differently. In partic-ular, the core cannot be treated in the same way as employees in the traditional organisation. They do not respond well to autocratic, top-down management. They need to be consulted, be involved in decision making and allowed to get on with their jobs within their areas of expertise. The relationship is that of colleague to colleague rather than employer to employee.

Some training organisations with which we are familiar are structured this way. There is a core of full-time staff who organise and promote the training events. Trainers, desk top publishers, printers, venues and audio-visual requirements are outsourced. There is also a flexible labour force of training assistants, word processor operators and clerical assistants to help at peak times.

One of the trends is that a significant proportion of the second and third leaves of the shamrock, the contractors and flexible labour force, are women. This type of organisation suits many women as it allows them to organise working hours to suit themselves or to work from home. And the style of management required in the shamrock organisation—with its emphasis on communication, nego-tiation, flexibility and responsibility—is also more compatible with feminine values.

So . . . the move away from an industrial manufacturing base towards the era of the information super highway and beyond requires a paradigm shift—not only in values and organisation structure but also in the basic fabric of the beliefs of developed societies. As the shift brings work values closer to natural feminine values for the first time, it is likely that it will also open the doors to female leadership. Inevitably, the effect of significant numbers of women at levels of power and influence will change our approach to management and leadership, and possibly change the very nature of the 'game' as we have known it.

What we envisage as we move into the twenty-first century is that all positions will become just as accessible to women as they are now to men, that the generic 'he' will disappear from business language as irrelevant, and that organisations will become places where all employees can find fulfillment, enjoyment and a sense of purpose and achievement.

GLASS CEILING AND BEYOND

While the vision is in place, there is still more spadework to be done before it can become a reality. As we have seen, initiatives of the 1970s and 1980s have led to women being increasingly represented in organisations—at the lower levels and into middle management.

But moving into levels of power and influence in significant numbers is proving another hurdle for women to overcome. There is still a barrier, the 'glass ceiling', which, up until now, has prevented most women from entering the senior levels of organisations and the corporate boardrooms.[8]

Could it be that this glass ceiling has become a self-imposed limitation? Is it that women are not capable? Is it because we don't want to hack the pace? Or is there something else, like our values, or the values and cultures of the organisations for which we work, or the values of the societies in which we live, that is stopping us? Or is it purely a function of patriarchal values and male domination?

Julie's story . . .

Now I know what the glass ceiling feels like. I am the most senior female in my organisation, reporting directly to the CEO. Some people might think that I have broken through the glass ceiling, but it certainly doesn't feel like it to me.

Eighteen months ago I was passed over in favour of an external appointment. Bill (he was male, of course) knew our CEO through one of his networks, and had obviously impressed him by his contacts in the industry. These contacts proved about as solid as jelly. And, to make matters worse, Bill had an old-fashioned, autocratic management style which he tried to impose on a highly professional and efficient work group.

After a disastrous and stressful 12 months which saw the productivity of the group slip dangerously, Bill saw the writing on the wall and resigned. With obvious reluctance I was given his job.

Immediately the doors of the old boys' network snapped shut. I am included in the regular weekly meetings of the executive group, but subtly excluded from committees, meetings and decisions around the functioning of other divisions and of the organisation as a whole. I don't receive copies of reports that go to all the other executives and miss out on special briefings and discussions. And I am still subject to ad hoc and autocratic decision making by the CEO.

There are positives. Our bottom-line results, on which we are measured by the CEO, are excellent. I am receiving great support from my team, and in general from other women in the organisation. As the organisation is a traditional, bottom-line focused, male-dominated workplace, all women employees (from managers to sales representatives to secretaries) experience the subtle discrimination that inevitably follows.

I'm not sure what the future holds for me. I'll fight on for a while, but there comes a point when the fight just isn't worth it.

Out of sheer necessity, women have been accepted at the lower levels of organisations. But a senior position, which allows input into the strategy and future direction of an organisation, is only entrusted to someone with the 'right' experience, the 'right' contacts, and who shares similar work values—and that person is usually another male. We all have a tendency to appoint people who are like us. And, in general, the more senior the appointment, the more similar is the successful new executive to existing senior managers. So men keep getting the plum positions!

As we see it, the critical issue for the 1990s and into the twenty-first century is that we need a new, a different approach. Organisational values must change if we are going to run businesses successfully in a global economy. It is no longer a question of whether men will allow women in at senior levels. Organisations need what women have to offer, as the values of women are more closely aligned to those needed by organisations both now and into the forseeable future. And so, as a matter of economic survival, business needs women at the most senior and influential levels.

STRATEGIES FOR WOMEN

The question then becomes—what strategies should women adopt to break through this invisible barrier, the glass ceiling? How can we move into more strategic leadership roles in organisations?

One way is for women to simply model men and become 'female men', discarding our innate feminine principles and values. This has worked and still does work for some women, but it would seem to be an unwise strategy for large numbers of women to adopt, given that the trend in the information economy and the emerging organisation is for more emphasis on feminine values.

The essential point is that women and men are different. We tend to have different values and, as we will see in later chapters, our brains are organised differently and our beliefs, attitudes, experiences, conditioning and hormones are different. It is only as women have entered the male-dominated business arena that some women have adopted the strategy of operating in the same way as men, in order to gain acceptance. But we are not the same, and we are neither superior nor inferior, better nor worse. We are different! In the past, this difference has worked to the disadvantage of women in business. It is now our strength. Our very difference from men will give us those critical distinctions for the future on how to do business, how to relate to each other and our priorities both for ourselves and for planet Earth.

There are a number of strategies that women can follow to get themselves into positions of influence and power. One is to stay in traditional organisations and continue to exert pressure on the system from the inside. Another strategy is for women to move out of the traditional corporate world and set up our own businesses. Given the trends towards shamrock organisations identified by Charles Handy, this second strategy is not opting out but is a valid and powerful way to influence the 'game' of business as we know it.

Let's look at both these strategies.

Big business

The large organisations, including multi-national and public sector organisations, are still the major employers, and many women will continue to choose to work within their structures. To achieve a fulfilling career, they will need to believe that the skills and abilities they offer are complementary and of equal value to those offered by men. And if they want to move into more senior positions and influence the values, structures and strategies of organisations, women are going to have to take the initiative. To achieve a critical mass at senior levels they cannot sit back and continue to work quietly and efficiently and expect to be invited into senior management.

What will be useful in this process is for women to understand male values, as well as to be clear about their own, in order to make this blending of one organisational style into another a smooth and harmonious process. There are times when it is useful to adopt a male style (for example, motivating an all-male sales team, presenting a budget and forecast to the board), and yet it is important for women to be true to their own natural operating style and values in most day-to-day activities. Ultimately, operating any other way becomes too stressful, and this type of chronic stress can lead to physical illness and feelings that it is just not worth it.

One woman that we spoke with was very up-front about this. She had held a senior position in the public service for a number of years before deciding to set up her own consultancy. Her reason for the change was that playing the male 'game' was too stressful and she felt that she needed to be true to her own values in her work. A few years later, she is still convinced that she made the best decision for herself.

Some key ingredients are needed for success. Women must:

• acknowledge the importance of critical numbers of women becoming highly visible

• believe that women can become more powerful and influential. If we believe something strongly enough, we can turn belief into reality

• be committed to making it happen

• support each other.[9] There is no room for the 'tall poppy' syndrome in this process.[10] And this support is starting to happen. Increasingly, we are hearing of examples of women supporting each other in both large and small organisations.

Jane's story . . .

Jane had been with the organisation for three years as a state sales manager. During that time her group improved their performance markedly, and had become the most profitable regional area in the organisation.

The national sales manager resigned to take up another position, and Jane applied for the job. This position reported directly to the managing director, and a woman had never been appointed to this level of the organisation before.

She was actively encouraged in her application by her own team, head office staff (men as well as women), by state managers and by the (largely female) sales force across the country. This support took a variety of forms:

- face-to-face encouragement

- supportive phone calls from interstate

- networking

- letters and phone calls to the managing director

Nevertheless, there was considerable delay in making an appointment while the open market was searched for other possible candidates. It took nearly four months before Jane was confirmed in her new role.

This does not mean that all women should, or will, choose the path of senior management. What it does mean is that all women in business should believe that they have equal worth to men, should see themselves as leaders and influencers, and that they should strongly support and encourage the women who do set themselves the goal of moving into positions of power and influence.

Small business

There is another way for women—and this is the path of small business. Small organisations need to be flexible and innovative in order to survive. There is no room for reliance on status, hierarchical position, rigid rules and procedures. They can experiment with structures and leadership styles. And, as larger organisations continue the trend of downsizing and outsourcing more of their functions, they will come to rely on the smaller, more efficient organisations to provide many of their needs. Small business can lead by example!

Increasing numbers of women are making this choice.[11] In the US, 30 per cent of small businesses are owned by women; in the UK, Canada and Australia the percentage is even higher, and it is growing. For example, in Australia, the number of female business proprietors is growing at least 5 per cent faster than the number of male proprietors. And statistics are also starting to show that female-owned small businesses tend to be more profitable than those owned and operated by male proprietors. This is being achieved despite the many barriers still imposed on women by our patriarchal society— barriers of prejudice, traditional role expectations, lack of support and restricted access to finance.

Why are more and more women choosing to take the highly risky and often lonely path of setting up their own businesses? The reasons are many and complex. Conflicts between personal and corporate values, the inflexibility of large organisations, the difficulty women are experiencing in moving to the most senior levels of traditional organisations, the stifling of both their initiative and natural management style are all contributing factors. Women business owners can achieve balance and flexibility in their lives and the freedom to accommodate career, family and other important values.

Governments and big business are starting to recognise the potential of small business to influence the direction and profitability of economies. And the women who choose this path are beginning to exert considerable pressure on the patriarchal business system to become more responsive to change and become more people- as well as profit-focused. Many of these women have had experience in large organisations and now as entrepreneurs, specialists and consultants are going back into the organisations which would not promote them and showing them how to operate successfully in today's rapidly changing and often chaotic business environment.

Dianne's story . . .

Dianne was a manager with a multi-national high technology organisation. It was a traditional, male-dominated bureaucracy and values were strongly based on playing by the rules and doing things in the established way.

At her annual performance appraisal Dianne was rated 'excellent' in each of the key categories (achievement of financial objectives, planning, communication, motivation and development of staff, etc.). And yet her manager, in the category 'Likely next job or career step', marked her 'Unsuitable for further promotion'. When Dianne questioned this, he replied: 'I'm just not comfortable with your management style—with the way you do things. It doesn't fit in with our culture.'

What was her management style? It was people-focused. Dianne believed (and still believes) that results are achieved through people.

Dianne left the organisation. With a partner, she has now been running her own business for twelve years, offering advice on management and structural problems to organisations, including her old company.

A comment that has frequently been made to us by women who have chosen to go into business for themselves is that they find freedom for the first time to express their natural values. Ironically this often includes values which would normally be considered 'masculine', such as independence, competitiveness and achievement. These behaviours exist in many women (in Carl Jung's terms as part of the *animus*)[12] but are often repressed in the largely male-dominated traditional work environment.

There appear to be at least two influencing factors here. One is the system that expects women to behave in a certain way. The second is that, until recently, women themselves have not been willing to own their *animus*. This is just the same as many men who are not willing to admit to their *anima*—the feminine qualities which exist in the male persona. We each have the ability to develop more of the other's values and qualities and we now have the tools and know-how to do this if we choose. (See the exercise on 'How to change your values' on pages 190–1.)

IN SUMMARY

Values drive our actions. They drive men to compete, to achieve, to aim for power and to focus on success and control. They drive women towards love, harmony and nurturing and to focus on people and relationships.

We acquire these values from our conditioning, our environment, our culture and our biological make-up. For women, the message is clear. We live in a male-dominated world where the macro models of independence and status are men, and the female models tend to reflect subservience, acceptance and passivity. This equips women for a domestic role, but not for a career, except at the lowest levels of the corporate world.

But things are changing. We now know how to identify and change our values, so that we can choose to have the values that complement our innermost needs and desires. And for increasing numbers of women, the balance of a family and a successful career is becoming important.

Things are also shifting at the corporate level. Traditional organisational values are gradually changing in the new environment of rapid technological change and socio-economic uncertainty. And they are moving in the direction of feminine values.

It is both inevitable and desirable that more women move into positions of influence and high visibility. And we believe that there is another simple ingredient, very closely linked to values, that can accelerate the emergence of female leaders. This ingredient may have become the missing link for a lot of women, especially those of us who have continually battled in the face of adversity when working in male-dominated hierarchical organisations . . .

3

SELF-FULFILLING PROPHECIES . . .

Our beliefs are our choice. You can choose the beliefs that
support you and you can choose the ones that limit you and
hold you back.

Anthony Robbins[1]

. . . BELIEFS

Many women believe that change is possible and necessary, yet there
is still some doubt that women are capable of leading the change.
Sure, some very successful women have made it to executive positions in various industries today. 'But at what price?' is often the
question asked.

As we have seen, corporate values are starting to change in
response to the needs of the information age and the global economy, and to change in a way that is more compatible with natural
female values. Hopefully this will gradually mean that a lot more
women will start to believe that we, together with men, can become
the leaders of the future. But this natural evolution needs to be
accelerated. Women can speed up the process, but in order to do
this, we are going to have to adopt some different strategies. This
process always starts with belief—the belief that we are able to
choose to do something differently.

What are beliefs?

Beliefs are closely linked to values but tend to be closer to our conscious awareness than values. Figure 3.1 carries the analogy of the tree further. Where the deepest unconscious influencers of our behaviour are represented by the tree trunk and values are represented by the main branches, beliefs form the sub-branches and twigs.

Figure 3.1

While values govern our judgments about good and bad, right and wrong, beliefs are statements about how we feel about the world.

Our beliefs are generated from a number of sources, including:

- our environment—family, school, work

- past experiences and results

- information we have gained

- acknowledgments we have received

- thinking about future imagined occurrences[2]

In order to make sense of all of these sources we attach meaning to them in the form of statements which we call beliefs. In other words, we build our beliefs by generalising from our experiences, our environment and our contact with other people. What we find is that our beliefs either reinforce old values or help us to create new ones. For every past, present and future imagined event or experience in our life we tend to associate at least one belief to it so that it has meaning for us.

Here are some examples of how beliefs might be adopted:

As a young girl Sally was bitten by a small dog. Ever since then she has had a belief that all dogs will bite her.

For many years men have been taught to believe that displaying emotions like sadness, grief and crying is a sign of weakness and is unmasculine. Today we know from medical research that pent-up and suppressed emotions can actually be disease-forming and that release of emotions can very often assist in the cure of disease. Despite this evidence many men still hold to the belief that crying is a woman's domain. Strong men don't cry after all!

After a long line of male appointments to the positions of advertising manager and assistant advertising manager, a woman was appointed to the position of advertising manager. Most people believed that it was a token appointment. Few actually believed that the woman was promoted on merit. This appointment merely reinforced the belief that this particular organisation was committed to keeping the top jobs for the boys. Which, by the way, it still does.

For some years before she reached the position of human resources manager, Yvonne had a clear picture of herself in this role. Her strong sense of visioning had created the positive belief that she was capable of fulfilling this executive level position. However, on becoming human resources manager, she accepted a lower salary package than the seven other executive managers. This limiting belief about her own self-worth had two significant effects. It reinforced existing organisational beliefs that women should be paid less than men, and it also disadvantaged her department because none of her staff earned as much as their equivalents in other departments.

> *BELIEFS*
> *ARE*
> *NOT*
> *TRUTHS* [3]

For the time that a belief is a strong motivating force in our lives we tend to attach an inflexible truth to that belief. Unfortunately, the trap that many of us fall into is that we hold that all beliefs are truths. Now this may not be such a bad thing if the belief is a positive motivating force propelling us to achieve what we want. What happens, though, when it's a limiting belief, one that prevents us from reaching our goals? What would happen if, because of centuries of male domination, women did not believe that they could take on influential and highly visible roles?

The point is . . . if the beliefs we have had about ourselves until now have not provided us with a representative proportion of females at the executive levels of organisations, then it's time to change them. This change must begin at an individual level and the first stage of the process is awareness. Awareness that a belief is a powerful guiding force for getting what we want. And, more importantly, awareness of what our beliefs actually are.

Reframing your beliefs

Here are some simple steps to help you understand and reframe your beliefs:

- Become aware of your own beliefs.

    Notice the beliefs that empower you and the ones that limit you. Table 3.1 sets some of these out.

Table 3.1

Empowering beliefs	Limiting beliefs
No matter what, I know I can make it.	There's no hope.
I've earned the right to be promoted.	I can't manage anyone
I'm as good as the next person.	I'm too fat/ugly/old/young/inexperienced.
I know I can do a great job.	Men are better at business than women.
Working with other executives will be challenging and fun.	I'll have to give up my personal life for a career.

Which list do you think is going to motivate you the most?

In fact, the chances are that any of the above beliefs will motivate you equally. Limiting beliefs will motivate you negatively and empowering beliefs will motivate you positively. To motivate yourself positively on a consistent basis you must surround yourself by empowering beliefs. And you can make a conscious choice to do this.

- Frame your beliefs in the positive.

    Restate your limiting beliefs in the positive and in a way that supports you and your efforts. For example 'I can't manage anyone' could become 'I did a great job of . . .' and 'There's no hope' may become 'I can still turn this around if I . . .' and so on.

Take every opportunity to reinforce your new beliefs. Also notice if they are working or not. If they're not working for you then you may need to look at changing a value or the ordering of your values.

Liz's story . . .

I have been a primary school teacher for 25 years and always felt that I wasn't bright enough to do a university degree. Two years ago it became a necessity. My salary was not going to move any higher and I would not be able to achieve a greater level of professionalism if I did not have a degree.

I applied to a university to begin a degree in education by correspondence. I was still unsure of my ability, but felt that it was worth a try. I received help, support and encouragement from my mother and close friends and they gave me the belief that I could achieve.

The first semester was the toughest. I just didn't know whether my standard was good enough. After a couple of 'distinctions' I gained more confidence. I knew that if I continued to apply myself I could achieve it.

I finished the degree last September, with 'distinction' passes or higher in all subjects. I now have been accepted to do a Master's degree and I am looking forward to this, as I know it will be challenging and stimulating.

Someone once said: 'Whether you think you can or you think you can't, either way you're right'. You can create your own reality through your beliefs. For example, in writing this book, we consciously developed some strong empowering beliefs:

- we could write a book better together than separately

- the researching and writing would be a fun process

- the books that we needed to consult would be there at the right time for us

- ideas and words would jump out at us when we needed them

- if we just got something—anything—on to paper, the words we needed would flow from that

These beliefs became our reality and, without fail, worked for us.

COMING TO THE SURFACE

Coming back to the metaphor of the tree, let's take a look at the leaves.

Figure 3.2

The leaves represent our **attitudes**, yet another aspect of our personality and behaviour derived directly from our values and beliefs. Our attitudes are more conscious than our beliefs, which in turn are more conscious than our values.

What are attitudes?

Our attitudes are picked up by other people in our verbal and non-verbal behaviour in a specific situation.

> Mary is ringing a major supplier to confirm her acceptance of their training proposal valued at $150 000. The receptionist answers the phone and puts Mary through to her contact. The phone is answered with a curt 'Hello'.
> Mary says, 'Is that you, Peta?'
> 'No.' A pregnant pause follows.
> 'This is Mary Harrington. Is Peta available, please?'
> 'No.'
> By this time, Mary is feeling irritated. She says, 'I'd like Peta to call me back. Would you please take a message?'
> There is a definite 'tssk' in the reply, 'Yeah.'
> 'Would you please ask Peta to call Mary Harrington on . . .'
> 'Hang on.' This is clearly a very inconvenient request. 'I'll have to go and get a pen.'
> Another pause, and then, 'What's your name?'
> And so on.

This scenario shows how clearly a person's attitude is communicated over a telephone by their choice of words and tone of voice. Mary was left in no doubt that whoever answered the phone was inconvenienced and considered the phone call to be an unwelcome interruption.

Even without words, attitudes can be conveyed very powerfully. Notice the behaviours of people who are in 'service type' jobs. How is it that you can distinguish between a 'can do' and a 'won't do' attitude almost instantaneously? What is it about attitudes that do not need words to be conveyed?

Next time you go out for a cup of coffee or a meal, notice the attitude of the person who is serving you. Are they coming from 'can do' or 'won't do?' How do you know this? Are their words consistent with their attitude?

Notice when a person's attitude and words are inconsistent. What influences your assessment of that person's attitude—their words or their behaviours?

Stereotypes

Leonie Still is an Australian academic who has researched and written extensively on women in business. In her book *Winning the Corporate Battle*, she gives a good example of people's attitudes to business men and business women. We have borrowed from and adapted her list in table 3.2.[4]

Table 3.2

A business woman is:	A business man is:
aggressive	dynamic
picky	good on detail
bitchy	apt to lose his temper
pushy	a go-getter
moody	depressed
stuck-up	confident
hard as nails	firm
stubborn	a man of his convictions
obsessive	persistent
a lush	able to handle his liquor
emotional	human
power hungry	career conscious
secretive	diplomatic
impulsive	a quick decision maker
hard to work for	tough but fair

Stereotypes which grow out of these attitudes have been used in the business world to stifle the development of women. Women who have become successful have been given labels such as 'Queen Bee', 'Iron Maiden', 'Dragon', 'Bitch' . . . just to name a few.

Cheryl's story . . .

My first job was as a typist in the typing pool of a large office. My boss was the office services supervisor, and she was commonly known as 'the Dragon'.

She always seemed to be breathing down our necks. She knew when we were slacking or spending too long in the ladies room. And she wouldn't let any work leave the typing pool unless she had checked it. She never missed anything.

Looking back, I can understand her better now. We were more interested in boys and parties than work but, to her, work was a career. It was important to her to do the best job she could, and the only way she could do that was by being tough with us all the time.

Covert discrimination against women is a reflection of attitudes, which in turn reflect beliefs and values about the role of women. Subtle put-downs are commonly experienced by women in business. For example, the contribution in the meeting that is ignored, the chance reference to 'birds', the use of the word 'girls' when referring to female staff, the jesting reference to a pretty face, or great legs.

Roma's story . . .

I held a management position in a multi-national company for 3 years. During that time:

- interstate air travel was always a major justification exercise, that is, it took a number of meetings each time to convince executive management that it was necessary

- on one interstate trip I was 'allowed' to go as long as the state manager I was visiting provided my accommodation (she was also a female)

- any company-paid training that I attended required a series of meetings and justifications

When I resigned, I made several recommendations about maintaining momentum in my team. My suggestions included appointing existing staff to promotion positions. Each of these suggestions was ignored in the short term.

Against my recommendations, a replacement for my position was found from outside the organisation. He was a male, with no previous experience in our industry and, as the team discovered, he had an autocratic management style totally out of step with what they had been used to. My colleagues informed me that he managed to alienate himself from most people in the office other than the executive management, who appeared to be blind to his failings. On appointment:

- he was immediately included in regular executive management meetings to which I had seldom been invited

- he was flown to key offices interstate as part of his induction

- he was immediately sent on company-sponsored training courses

It took 3 months for management to admit to his ineptitude and ask him to resign.

Not long after his departure, some of my previous recommendations were implemented. In particular, one of my team (a female) was appointed as team manager and, guess what?

- she received no salary increase with her promotion

- she was not included in the regular executive management meetings

- she was not flown interstate to develop relationships with the other key offices

- any company-sponsored training she received was on a 50/50 basis

Unfortunately, despite all the advances women have made so far, discrimination is still alive and kicking, especially at the higher levels of many organisations. The prevailing attitude is still that men should be senior managers.

High expectations

In addition to experiencing discrimination, women continue to face subordinates who often expect more of female bosses than of male bosses. They expect them to be considerate, to listen, to be even-handed, to accept defeat gracefully and to be able to represent their interests forcefully. A male boss, in general, is allowed to be more authoritarian and unapproachable, and a more aggressive reaction to set backs is condoned. Subordinates are also tougher on female managers who fall down in any of these areas.

As Natasha Josefowitz claims:

> Women who wish to move up need to become exquisitely per-ceptive evaluators of how far to push the norms and how fast. We need to tread the fine line between not meeting others' expectations of how women should behave, yet not upsetting people to such a degree that our objective is never reached.
>
> The task becomes a matter not of breaking the stereotypes but of how and when to do it. For career-oriented women, respecting male expectations of what 'female' behaviour is like is not only self-defeating in terms of opportunities to advance, but also in terms of opportunities to change norms, modify stereotyp-ing, and diminish discrimination.[5]

V-B-A CHAIN

As we have seen, our attitudes are often more obvious to others than the beliefs and values that underpin them. And since we now know that stereotypes and attitudes are just the surface reflection of beliefs and values, it is important to establish the links between them.

Imagine that values, beliefs and attitudes are all connected together in the same way that links form a chain. We call it the V-B-A chain!

Do any of the examples in table 3.3 sound familiar to you? No doubt you can think of plenty more from your own experience. (Try the exercise on page 192.)

So how do we change the stereotypes and break the disempower-ing V-B-A chains?

Up until now, attempts have been made through legislation (Equal Opportunity and Affirmative Action legislation, Anti-Dis-crimination boards), court action (for example, on sexual

Table 3.3   V-B-A chain

Most obvious		Least obvious
Attitudes	Beliefs	Values
indifference, condescension towards and exclusion of women managers	a woman's place is in the home	patriarchal work ethic
positive outlook, responsible approach	I can	High self-worth
conformity to the system with a 9-to-5 mentality: 'I'm only working to help pay off the mortgage.'	the price of a career is too high . . . I'll have to sacrifice family and relationships	family loyalty or a need to be taken care of

harassment), and through assertiveness and other training specifically for women. And things have improved for women in business over the last twenty years. We *are* now accepted as professionals and as managers. Other women and men are growing accustomed to having women as their bosses. The efforts of the feminist movement are paying off.

But there is still a lot further to go. We have merely scratched the surface of women's potential and contribution. For example:

- Women are not yet adequately represented as business leaders and CEOs. Our minuscule presence at this critical level of business has barely changed over the last twenty years.

- There is still a belief among many women that they can only succeed if they become 'female men'. And this puts many women off; they don't think it is worth the sacrifice.

As one woman who has succesfully combined both a family and a career said to us:

I find that young women today are either giving up all idea of a career—they're finding it all too hard—or they're deciding not to have families and to go for it in a really male way. I'm not comfortable with either of these choices, but I don't know what else to advise them to do.[6]

ANOTHER WAY

There *is* another way. We don't have to become female men, and we don't have to give up. Women must be themselves and be confident that what they have to offer is valuable. We are not the same as men, and it is only when we acknowledge that differences do exist that we can start to value the untapped potential that lies in all of us. We have a different way of dealing with people, of perceiving problems and opportunities, of decision making, of leading.

In fact, in many ways it is possible for women to have the best of both worlds. Through understanding our own natural way of operating, and through modelling the operating styles of others (males as well as females), we can give ourselves more behavioural choices and thus greater flexibility in our work and management styles. We will look at this in more detail in chapters 5 and 8.

In the early days of feminism, the cry was for equality. It was felt necessary to minimise the differences between women and men as 'difference' meant a less valued, an inferior, role for women. Women were still seen, as Simone de Beauvoir put it, as the 'second sex'.[7] We were expected to be less able than men, to carry out 'less important' functions, to be child carers and housewives and to be subservient to and dependent on men. The old image of the wife in the home, barefoot and pregnant, was still too close for comfort. And this picture is still true in many parts of the world.

Over the last twenty years in the West and in some parts of Asia the change in the attitudes of women has been nothing short of dramatic. In general we now expect to work, have greater self-esteem, are more independent, and are irritated and more vocal when we are not treated as equals.

Men's attitudes, understandably, are changing more slowly, although changes are certainly happening at the middle class, professional level. A recent newspaper article highlighted the fact that in the middle class in Australia there are now more marriages of professionals and 'more-or-less' financial equals and that more and more middle-class families have two incomes.[8] For other women, the stark reality remains that their incomes are still lower than their male equivalents.[9] Even where we are recognised as professionals we are still not quite equivalent to a male professional.

> *'The past decade has seen the steady advance of women into new areas, the work-process itself has begun to move in a more feminine-friendly direction, and men's attitudes have begun to budge.'*
>
> Martin Jacques[10]

The next stage in the change process must come from women—from our values, beliefs and attitudes about our abilities, about what we can do and about what we can become. If we believe in ourselves and our potential strongly enough, and act on that belief, then we can influence other people, and whole systems, to change. If we believe something strongly enough we can make that belief a reality.

Kerry's story . . .

I have two grown-up sons. I have brought them up alone since they were 3 and 5 years old respectively, and they have grown up in a female-dominated household with a mother who was the only income earner. My friends (both women and men) also tend to be career focused.

My sons' experience and their reality leads them to expect women, just as much as men, to be capable, independent decision makers and leaders. In fact, they find it difficult to understand women who choose to stay at home as dependants.

A female leader in a world that is traditionally male is Grace M. Atkinson the executive vice-president and chairman, Hong Kong/China, of J. Walter Thompson, one of the largest advertising agencies in the Asia-Pacific region. Her thoughts on how she has made it to a position occupied by few women in business are illuminating:

It's all a matter of attitude, thinking positively and thinking of winning and not losing. And it does take high self esteem! A lot of women are outwardly aggressive and pushy but really underneath there's a lot of fear. It's this fear that people sense and therefore they don't get to the top. To get rid of the fear we need to look at what we are afraid of and conquer it.

Try to be yourself. Acknowledge your wins. Look at what didn't work and learn. Since I did that for myself, I have been managing myself better and I therefore have time to do what I am good at and still have time to do other things. My life has more balance now.

Women make too much of not getting equal billing with men in top positions . . . but they don't realise that it takes a lot of energy. Women do not have to be the victim—it's our choice to play this role.[11]

IN SUMMARY

Our beliefs are self-fulfilling prophesies. If we believe we can do something, then we can; if we believe we can't, then we can't. For women this is especially relevant. Unless we believe in ourselves, then we won't succeed. We need to consciously frame our beliefs in the positive and create our own reality through empowering beliefs.

Attitudes and stereotypes are the surface reflection of values and beliefs. They are more obvious than the values and beliefs that lie beneath them. We notice discriminatory attitudes and behaviours and tend to react to them, whereas it is the V-B-A chain that needs to be broken. And the first chains to break are our own, by constructing empowering V-B-A chains for ourselves.

We have come a long way. We now have some understanding of the part our values, beliefs and attitudes play in our lives. And there are still other influencing factors in our make-up that we need to look at in considering and valuing the differences between women and men.

Until ten years ago, behavioural differences between women and men were always explained by social conditioning. The role of biology and the human brain were not considered as influential factors in shaping female and male behaviour. Even today, most people still regard the environment and social conditioning as the key determinants of gender specific behaviour.

Let's take a closer look . . .

4

BRAIN SEX . . .

'She said to him
The academic life must be pleasant—
you're a professor, how nice.
He said to her
Well, maybe some day
you'll marry one.
She said to him,
Why should I marry one
when I can be one.'

Natasha Josefowitz[1]

. . . VERSUS CONDITIONING

Many of us live our lives seldom questioning the status quo in terms of gender behaviour. From birth and through a conditioning and socialising process as we develop we seldom question that 'this is how boys and men should behave and this is how girls and women should behave'. When the status quo is questioned or renegades who behave contrary to the norm emerge, the consequences have typically been ostracism, loneliness or cult following, among a few options!

The traditional socialisation process of most countries has until now placed women at a disadvantage in the world of business. Carolyn Brand, the first female to reach the rank of commander in the Royal Australian Navy, feels strongly about this:

> One of the things girls are conditioned to as children is not to be rough, to be quiet and decorous, and we lose a great deal as a result. When the element of rough and tumble, push and shove, gets knocked out of you early as a female, then you lose a lot of your personal confidence in dealing with physical situations. It's that inability to push forward and take charge of whatever the situation is and deal with it that is so detrimental to females being seen as being able to carry out jobs equally with men.[2]

47

Consider a common scenario for women and men who were conditioned by pre-1960s values . . .

It's a boy

The midwife announces 'It's a boy, it's a boy' and the proud parents from then on say words to the effect of 'Isn't he handsome', 'Look at those strong hands', 'He's got a voice as big as his dad's'.

His parents call him Billie. As he develops he's dressed in blue and other clothes designed to readily identify him as a little boy. The toys he's given are bears, balls, trucks, guns, dinkies, footballs and boats. He's encouraged to play outside and when he gets into rough and tumble games his parents smile and say, 'Boys will be boys'.

Billie is handled more roughly, especially by his dad and other male relatives, than if he were a little girl. When he cries he's told, 'Don't be such a baby', and 'Only sissies cry'.

As time goes on Billie plays football in winter and cricket in summer. He learns to tackle hard and play aggressively. This is reinforced by coaches, parents and friends on the sidelines. Winning is all that matters—winning at all costs. When Billie does something against the rules, such as a head high tackle, and gets away with it, he becomes a hero to his team-mates.

At school, Billie is encouraged to take 'important' subjects like maths, physics, chemistry and economics because these will stand him in good stead for a career. It's made very clear to him that drama, music and art are diversions, unless he happens to have an outstanding talent in one of these, in which case he is pushed into it in order to develop a career.

Billie's environment—his parents, relatives, school, peer group, media, television, work colleagues, etc.—consistently reinforces 'manly' behaviour. His models for living remind him constantly of what is important—work, career, competition, winning, aggression, becoming the breadwinner, and so on. Part of this involves Billie, who now prefers to be called Bill, learning to look on girls and females in general as weaker, gentler, emotional, dependent beings who require protection.

It's a girl

When the midwife announces 'It's a girl, it's a girl', the scenario tends to be radically different. The proud parents say words like 'Isn't she beautiful', 'Look at those cute curls,' and 'She's got a mouth just like her mother's'.

Her parents call her Suzie. She's dressed in pink with lots of frills and bows to identify her as a little girl. The toys she is given are dolls, soft cuddly toys, a tea set, doll's house and pram, and she's encouraged to help her mother around the home and taught to avoid boisterous games that might dirty or tear her clothes.

Suzie is handled more gently than if she were a boy, especially by male relations. When she cries she is consoled and cuddled and told 'There, there, it's okay', and then given a special treat.

As time goes on Suzie goes to singing and dance classes and to the gym. She learns to be ladylike, that posture is important and that competition provides healthy exercise. Winning is not the only thing—it's the activity and the way it's done that are emphasised.

Suzie is encouraged to read as a pastime and is taught to sew by her mother. At school, the subjects she takes reflect an 'all round education' and good grades are not downplayed. In general she is steered more into the social sciences rather than the general sciences, and her education includes needlework, music, art, drama and physical education. Because she is bright, she is expected to go to university to complete her education, and also because she is likely to meet the 'right' kind of boy there.

All the influences in her environment reinforce 'feminine' behaviour. Her models for living emphasise the importance of family, caring, nurturing, organising a home, child-rearing and supporting her husband's career aspirations. Part of this involves an active husband-seek so that she can be cared for. Men are seen as being stronger, more independent, caretakers and heads of the household.

Conditioning is a strong influence in our lives. Sometimes the conditioning is overt, for example, 'Girls don't/shouldn't/can't . . .'. Sometimes it is so subtle that we only realise it later when someone points it out to us.

Women's names are a case in point. Until recently, the prefixes given to women reflected their marital status—'Miss' or 'Mrs'. The majority of women still adopt their husband's family name when they marry, and it was not so long ago that a woman's name was absolutely defined by her husband, for example, Mrs George Jones, Princess Michael of Kent. It is still only in the business world that the neutral 'Ms' is accepted as a female prefix, just as 'Mr' is a neutral male prefix.

The conditioning we receive tends to push women into roles that the patriarchy has defined as less influential and less visible—the roles of wife, housewife, mother, carer and nurturer. Look at the word 'mother'. It still carries connotations of the person responsible for the wellbeing of the family, while the word 'father' means—to most people—the provider of income.

> *'We tend to give*
> *our girls roots*
> *and our boys wings.'*
> Philip Zimbardo[3]

Suzie's dilemma

So how does someone like Suzie, who has been socialised for her role in the domestic world, fit into the world of business? The economic scene has changed since she was born. She has to earn her own living and she's expected to operate in the same business world as Bill. How does she do it?

Although things are gradually changing, the model of a typical Western business still tends to be patriarchal, as shown in the values of the traditional organisation in chapter 2 (see page 19). This model values 'masculine' managerial styles and deprecates traditional feminine behaviours in the work environment. So the chances are that Suzie, unless she consciously modifies her values and behaviours, will only be accepted into organisations at the lower levels, and she probably won't do too well in climbing the corporate ladder or in reaching the boardroom table.

Even today, if you ask people about the characteristics of men and women, most will spontaneously come up with a list like the one in table 4.1.

Table 4.1 **Some commonly perceived characteristics of women and men**

Men	Women
logical	intuitive
strong	weak, timid
unemotional	emotional
aggressive	gentle, caring
assertive	submissive
decisive	indecisive
leaders	followers
independent	dependent
scientific	humanistic
rational	irrational
competitive	cooperative
objective	sensitive

Translate this stereotyping into the workplace where 'good' managers still tend to be described as having the following characteristics:

aggressive, competitive, just, firm, rational and unemotional

and it is clear that Suzie, who is perceived as being more emotional, irrational, intuitive and dependent, is not considered to be good managerial material.

Potential contribution not realised

The accepted model in business does not value differences. Because of this the potential contribution that someone like Suzie can bring to the corporate world tends not to be realised.

> *'Ignorance, or denial, of difference*
> *has actually made the world*
> *a worse place for women.'*
> Anne Moir & David Jessel[4]

For years feminists have been fighting for gender neutral conditioning, feeling that only then could there be 'equality' between women and men. During the feminist years of the 1970s, any suggestion that there could be inborn, biological differences between women and men was regarded as a threat to this struggle for equality. But, as Christine Gorman says, 'biology has a funny way of confounding expectations'.[5] Over the past 30 years a lot has become known about hormones and genetic influences that contribute to our behaviours and to differences between women and men. It is now clear that there *are* biological and hormonal differences between women and men. The problem has been that, until now, the system has been skewed in favour of male preferences. It is time to remove the skew, to look at differences objectively and to value the contributions that both women and men can make.

So what do we now know about innate differences between women and men?

GENDER DIFFERENCES[6]

Current research indicates that differences between females and males show up at a very early age and that 'discernible, measurable differences in behaviour have been imprinted long before external influences have had a chance to get to work.'[7] For example, as babies girls are more interested in communicating with people and boys are more interested in objects; girls are less tolerant to sound, pain and discomfort, and are more sensitive to touch than boys. From an early age girls hold eye contact longer than boys. At this stage, conditioning has not yet had a chance to modify behaviour—these differences are 'wired into' our brains before birth.

Differences are also apparent very early on between the way girls and boys play. By the age of four, they usually play in single-sex groups. Girls choose playmates on the basis of friendship and liking, they are more inclusive of each other, their play involves turn taking and is more concerned with the process than with the outcome. Typical girls' activities include hopscotch, skipping and games such as families and schools, which are all involved with process and do not have a clear outcome and winner.

Until recently, the skills learnt by females in their games and activities have been seen as useful social and domestic skills but as irrelevant in the business world. This perception is gradually changing. In the highly uncertain and rapidly evolving world of the information age, the skills learnt by girls in their games—relationships, harmony, communication, flexibility, conflict resolution, negotiation, cooperation and improvisation—are increasingly valued. Girls' games 'do instill skills and attitudes that have value in the workplace—particularly in today's workplace, where innovation, entrepreneurship and creativity are in demand, and the authoritarian chain of command is increasingly obsolete'.[8]

Boys typically choose playmates because of their skills, use a larger space than girls for their activities, and have a lot of rough and tumble and physical contact in their games. Usually the outcomes of their games are clearly defined and there are winners and losers. In this way boys learn to accept rules, procedures and hierarchies and to focus on the outcome and winning. These activities equipped them very well for the demands of the industrial age, but it is questionable whether they will be as appropriate in the new business climate which is emerging from the accelerating waves of tehnological change.

Female and male brains

Also as a result of research, we know today that there are significant differences in the structure and organisation of typical female and male brains.

Some 30 years ago, in researching epileptics who had had part of their brains removed, a psychologist named Herbert Landsell found that:[9]

- males with right hemisphere brain damage performed badly on spatial skills tests, while the performance of females with similar brain damage was barely changed

- males with left hemisphere brain damage lost much of their language ability, while females with similar brain damage retained most of their language skills.

So Landsell's conclusion was that male brains have specific locations for language and spatial skills, while language and spatial skills are located in both hemispheres of the brain in females.

Since then, it has become clear that the typical male brain is more specialised and the typical female brain is more diffuse. That is, males tend to have specific centres for carrying out particular functions such as recognising words, mathematical calculations, sight and emotion. In the typical female brain these same functions are located in a number of centres, often in both hemispheres of the brain.

Table 4.2 summarises some of the key known differences between female and male brains.

Table 4.2   Brain organisation: the differences

Function	Brain location		Summary
	Men	Women	
Mechanics of language e.g. speech, grammar	Left hemisphere, front and back	Left hemisphere, front	Men more diffuse, women more specific
Vocabulary, defining words	Left hemisphere, front and back	Left and right hemispheres, front & back	Men more specific, women more diffuse
Visuo-spatial perception	Right hemisphere	Right and left hemispheres	Men more specific, women more diffuse
Emotion	Right hemisphere	Right and left hemispheres	Men more specific, women more diffuse

Source: Anne Moir and David Jessel, *Brain Sex*, Mandarin, London, 1989, p. 46.

The untapped potential

What does this mean in practice? At the simplest level, it means that women and men tend to do things and to think about things differently. At more complex levels, it may give women and men advantages (and disadvantages) in different areas. For example:[10]

- Women have more fibrous connections in the corpus collosum, connecting the left and right hemispheres, than men, which leads to the assertion that females can more readily process and use information from both hemispheres.

- Women tend to be better than men at recognising non-verbal nuances in voice, gesture, facial expression and a wide range of sensory information (perceptual ability).

- Girls tend to develop language skills earlier than boys and, throughout their lives, tend to be able to communicate more fluently.

- Women tend to be able to express and release emotion more easily than men.

- Women usually find language-related skills such as grammar, spelling and writing easier than men.

- Men tend to be able to process visual and spatial information more readily than women.

- Men also tend to have a greater capacity for mathematical reasoning.

- Men typically are able to focus more easily than women on a single task or problem.

It should be emphasised that these tendencies apply to 'typical' female and male brains. We all know examples of men with outstanding language skills and women who are brilliant at maths.

And it is also important to note that these findings are not yet universally accepted. A lot more research needs to be done on the effect of brain differences on the abilities, preferences and performance of women and men. What is clear, though, is that women and men do have different brain structures and preferences, and that this is one of the factors that causes us to think and act differently.

It seems that the human brain evolved during the millions of years that our ancestors spent in subsistence living and that this evolution occurred in response to tasks. So, for example, the female perceptual ability suited their subsistence roles of food gathering and preparing, nurturing and caring. The male visual and spatial ability fitted a hunting style of existence.

Although these role distinctions can still be seen in less developed economies in many parts of the world, they have little relevance today in the more developed Asian and Western worlds. And, of course, if the human brain has evolved over time, it makes sense that it is continuing to evolve in response to changing environments and changing tasks. However, brain preference does help us to understand why a stereotypical distribution of occupations still occurs between women and men, even though today, more than at any other time in history, many of us in the Western world have the luxury of choice. In other words, in selecting a career, people will tend to move towards their perceived or preferred strengths.

As a result, we continue to see more men in roles that typically match the male stereotype, as shown in table 4.3.

Table 4.3   Male stereotypical occupations

Mathematician	Scientist	Mechanic
Politician	Engineer	Architect
Banker	Accountant	Lawyer
Builder/Plumber	Technician	Astronaut
Chairman	CEO	Farmer
Executive	Bus driver	Pilot
Company director	Chef	Conductor
Factory worker	Dentist	Surgeon
Doctor	Programmer	

For women, the tendency is still towards occupations that fit the female stereotype.

Table 4.4   Female stereotypical occupations

Teacher	Nurse	Social worker
Secretary	Personnel officer	Midwife
Sales assistant	Cleaner	Hairdresser
Waitress	Actor	Telephonist
Receptionist	Beautician	Physiotherapist
Supervisor	Seamstress	Public relations
Childminder	Shop assistant	Trainer
Clerk	Housewife	Librarian
Bookkeeper	Word processor	Small business owner
First line manager		

Two key problems arise out of this gender stereotyping in terms of occupations. One is that, in our patriarchal culture, male stereotypical work has been valued, rewarded and remunerated more highly than female stereotypical work. A second, and equally important, problem is that men have, perhaps unconsciously, closed the doors to women in some areas in which they can make a significant contribution. One of these areas is leadership, and it is such an important area that we devote an entire chapter to it (see chapter 10).

The chances are that there will never be an equal distribution of women and men in professions like engineering, nursing and teaching. While there will always be women (who are as capable as men) in male stereotypical areas because of their brain preference, and men (who are as capable as women) in female stereotypical areas, it seems unlikely, on the information now available on brain preferences, that we will ever achieve an equal distribution of women and men throughout all occupations.

But there is no reason why we can't acknowledge the work of women and men equally. In a world that values differences, both female stereotypical and male stereotypical skills are needed. Spatial and mechanical skills, together with communication and relationship skills, are equally necessary. And we also need to look beyond the 'box'—to look at stereotypical male areas where women can make a useful contribution, and stereotypical female areas where men can make a useful contribution. Just because we have always looked at something in a particular way is not a good reason for continuing to look at it in the same way. In fact, it is the best possible reason for questioning it.

Opportunities for women

Many factors, including values, beliefs, attitudes and conditioning have until now been holding women back. And yet today, more than at any other time in history, the opportunities are there for women to grasp.

Why is this?

Because the workforce, organisational and management needs of the information age are very different from those of the industrial age, and they allow women to come into their own.

For a start, women are there in significant numbers in leading edge technologically based and service industries. And the sort of work they and their male colleagues are doing is different from the sort of work that people used to do. As John Naisbitt and Patricia Aburdene say, 'Mental tasks have replaced mechanical ones. "Work" is what goes on inside people's heads at desks, on airplanes, in meetings, at lunch. It is how they communicate with clients, what they write in memos, what they say at meetings'.[11]

It is easier for women to adjust to this new way of working than men. They don't have to unlearn old patterns of working and managing but can, for the first time, allow free rein to their preferences for flexibility, adaptation, communication and creativity. They are now well placed, especially given the needs of the information age, to break through the so-called 'glass ceiling' and achieve key positions in industries of the future.

HORMONAL INFLUENCES

Are the differences between women and men totally explained by conditioning and differences in brain structure?

The answer is an unequivocal NO. There is now solid scientific evidence that biochemistry also influences the structure and functions of the human brain at vital stages of development.[12]

At the time of conception, the sex of the foetus is supposedly determined by whether it receives an X or a Y chromosome from the father. Recent research has now confirmed that the structure of the brain until around the sixth week is female. To develop a male pattern, the brain is exposed to large doses of male hormone, testosterone, at 6 weeks. The absence of the male hormone determines whether the foetus continues to have a female brain pattern or not.

Things can go wrong in this process. Between the 'pure' female and 'pure' male patterns all sorts of combinations are possible. For example, a male foetus (XY) may not get a sufficient dose of male hormone to develop a male brain and male genitals, or it may get sufficient hormones to develop male sex organs but not enough to organise the brain into a male pattern. A female foetus (XX) may get a dose of male hormone at a critical stage that causes a male brain in a female body or male sex organs with a female brain. Research evidence suggests that 'the more male hormone the foetus is exposed to, the more the adult will be male in behaviour. The less the amount of male hormone, the more feminine the adult behaviour'.[13]

The male receives another large dose of male hormone at puberty and the female, from around the age of 8, begins to receive increased doses of the female hormones oestrogen and progesterone. It is from this time that differences in emotion, ambition, skill, aggression, aptitudes and behaviours between girls and boys become more apparent.

As we develop to adulthood, hormonal influences continue to play their part in behavioural differences. Figure 4.1 demonstrates the behaviours attributable to female and male hormonal influences.

It is important to realise that we can be anywhere on the continuum. While women tend to be bunched on the female side and men on the male side, in reality we all have varying amounts of female and male influences. So we can have women who are very competitive, self-confident and ambitious, and men who are caring, sensitive and empathetic.

Figure 4.1 Continuum of hormone influences

Continuum of hormonal influences

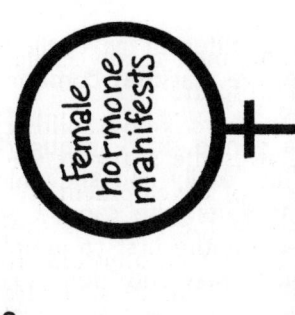

Male
hormone
manifests

Assertiveness
Aggression
Competition
Self-confidence
Single-mindedness
Concentration
Ambition
Independence

Shades and
variations exist
in between
to create

Female
hormone
manifests

Accommodation
Caring
Cooperation
Close relationships
Empathy
Broad focus
Nurturing
Interdependence

Judy's story . . .

I have two daughters who are as different as chalk and cheese. Sometimes it is hard to believe that they come from the same family.

My elder daughter, Jane, is a gentle, kind, thoughtful, stable person. People relate to her easily and she enjoys parties, dinners and any occasions when she can be with people. If someone needs help, Jane is the first to jump in.

When she was little, she loved to play with dolls. From an early age she enjoyed needlework, and she now makes most of her own and her daughters' clothes. Before she married Don she was a secretary. Now her children and Don, who is a high-flying business man, take up all her time.

Anne is two years younger than Jane. From the start she was fiercely independent and competitive. She wanted to feed herself as soon as she could hold a spoon. Anything Jane could do, Anne wanted to do. She was an outstanding sport at school, but school level competition was not enough for her. At the age of fourteen she was an A grade tennis player and reached the finals of the State Junior Championship.

She desperately wanted to go into acting, and worked for a year as a waitress to pay her fare to England. She was accepted into a prestigious English acting school. At the end of the course she married a fellow student, but arrived back home two years later with a baby and no husband. In her usual way, she declared that she would work things out for herself. She is now a drama teacher at the local high school and is doing a commerce degree part time.

IN SUMMARY

We now know that some of our behaviours are innate behaviours with which we enter the world, and others are learned and modified according to the experiences we have, our environment and other influences on us. There is a subtle interweaving throughout our lives of genetic influences, hormones and social conditioning. And, as we have seen, added to this are other influences like our values, beliefs and attitudes. Tables 4.5 and 4.6 summarise some of the key influences on women and men.

Table 4.5   Influences on females

Hormones influence	Brain sex determines	Social conditioning reinforces
nurturing need for caring and interdependence intuitive sense influencing language using suggestions and hints	verbal skills and language precision human interaction wholistic approach reading of nuances in behaviours and language of others ability to empathise	subordination of female roles tendency to undervalue occupations held by women

Table 4.6   Influences on males

Hormones influence	Brain sex determines	Social conditioning reinforces
aggression need for dominance sense of hierarchy and independence commanding, demanding language	spatial abilities mathematical and abstract reasoning preference for dealing with objects, machinery	dominant male culture high value placed on occupations undertaken by men

What is clear is that there are observable differences between women and men—differences in individual behaviour, experiences and outlook on life. These differences are so apparent that it has been said that we should regard women as beings from Venus and men as beings from Mars.[14] Or that we should consider women and men as coming from different cultures. And with this type of perspective we can certainly look more objectively at our respective strengths and weaknesses and the benefits to be gained by valuing our differences and combined contribution.

The differences between women and men translate into different aptitudes, abilities and preferences over a variety of life skills. Up until now these differences have been used to the advantage of males in general. The work and abilities of women have been discounted or undervalued even where the female ability—for example, for communication and cooperation—is a distinct advantage.

In a world of balance, the potential of each gender will be fully realised. We need to acknowledge the differences between women and men, and actively seek ways in which the contributions that can be brought by both women and men can be more effectively utilised.

At present, our institutions and culture do not accommodate the differences. Because of this women, especially women in business, have been forced to change in the direction of conforming to the male picture of the world. The male way of running organisations, managing people and developing resources is not the only way, and not necessarily the best way—it is just one possible way. What is now needed is a mutual or wholistic look at what is going to work best in the future for women *and* for men, *and* for the future condition of living on this planet.

> *'As long as we apply male*
> *egalitarian concepts to the*
> *understanding of the male and female*
> *relationships, we will continue to build*
> *mechanistic and inhumane societies.*
> *Life is enriched and intensified through the*
> *amplification of differences . . .*
> *What is needed is*
> *an acknowledgement of difference,*
> *but with no prejudiced attitudes*
> *of the superiority or inferiority of either sex.'*
> Robert Lawlor[15]

Once we acknowledge and value the differences between women and men and the contribution that each can bring to the work environment and the way we live, then we can begin to understand how we can best communicate with each other . . .

5

GENDER TALK . . . [1]

'Understanding the other's ways of talking is a giant leap
across the communication gap between women and men,
and a giant step toward opening lines of communication.'

Deborah Tannen[2]

. . . ARE WOMEN BEING HEARD?

Communication is a powerful tool for influencing others and in
achieving change, and women have several advantages in this area
over men. We tend to develop language earlier, have greater mastery
over the details of language, such as grammar and spelling, and use
communication as a means of negotiating conflicts and creating
harmony and intimacy.

And yet these natural advantages have not so far benefited women
in the business world. The differences that we have already seen
between women and men extend to communication—women and
men have, at an unconscious level, different assumptions about ways
of talking. Rather than being seen as an advantage, the natural female
style often seems to place us at a disadvantage in the business world,
an arena that has been dominated until now by the male rules of
hierarchy, aggressive competition and winning at all costs. For example, women tend to suggest rather than tell, say 'Let's' and 'Why don't
we?', and this has been seen as weak, indecisive and ineffective.

Pam's story . . .

I usually *ask* people to do things, rather than *tell* them. I
will say, 'Would you mind . . . ?' or 'Will you please . . .'.
My 14-year-old son objects to this. 'You're really telling me,
not asking me,' he says, 'so why don't you just tell me.'

Deborah Tannen, in her book *You Just Don't Understand*, claims that women and men speak different 'genderlects', and that talk between women and men is cross-cultural communication.[3] Women typically speak and hear a language of connection and intimacy and in their communication try to reach consensus, to minimise differences and avoid the appearance of superiority. Men, on the other hand, tend to speak and hear a language of status and independence and in their communication establish hierarchies and tell others what to do. This style has worked and continues to work in certain contexts, such as emergency situations and in combat.

The differences in styles are typically evident in situations that involve more than quick decision making skills. For example, something that occurs quite frequently in today's pressured business world is employee stress and upset. When someone becomes obviously upset (angry, tearful, disruptive, clumsy, prone to unusual mistakes), the communication strategies used to deal with the situation by male and female managers are usually quite different.

Typically, the male will offer a solution. He gives advice, while staying above and apart from the situation. Words like 'I know things are tough here right now but there is work to be done . . . that'll take your mind off things'. The female tends to empathise and perhaps share a similar personal experience. She puts herself at the same level as the employee, while the male retains the hierarchical distance. Most women intuitively feel that people need to *say* and to *share* what is happening for them before they can get on with their jobs effectively.

Observable differences

From as early as three years, differences in communication patterns between girls and boys are observable. As we saw in chapter 4, boys more often congregate in larger groups that are hierarchically structured, and play games that have elaborate systems of rules, and winners and losers. They tend to give orders and argue and interrupt each other a lot.

Girls play in smaller, more intimate groups (often just with a 'best' friend) without a hierarchical structure. Their games are non-competitive and encourage participation rather than winning and losing. And their language tends to be non-confrontational and inclusive, and instructions are expressed as suggestions. The effect of conditioning reinforces the natural tendency of female communication. Girls may be actively discouraged from expressing themselves forcefully, and so 'acquire speech habits that communicate uncertainty, hesitancy, indecisiveness and subordination'.[4]

So how can women communicate more effectively in the business world?

One way is by learning and adopting the male 'genderlect'. Certain women have found this to be easy and comfortable, because it allows them to integrate into the business world. However, learning the male genderlect offers no guarantees of success because of the gender bias in our system. This bias often results in women receiving lower salaries and slower promotion paths than men and being placed in 'off-line' or 'dead-end' positions. Take Yvonne, whom we mentioned in chapter 3, as an example:

Yvonne's story . . .

Yvonne adapted well to the male business world, learned to speak the jargon and achieved the executive position of human resources manager. However, this was the end of the line for her in the organisational structure. In her company, HR was considered an 'off-line' function, receiving a lower salary than a line function. There was no chance of her moving to the next level of the organisation, that of general management, because of her perceived lack of relevant business experience.

Adopting the male genderlect may also result in women being misunderstood by both men and other women.[5] Michael Grinder gives an example of this when he looks at female and male listening styles. The stereotypical male, when listening, sits back, his body is still, and he is silent. The stereotypical female listener leans forward, nods and makes cooperative sounds. When a female adopts the male listening style, this is typically interpreted by a male speaker as sterile and unfeminine, while a female speaker will feel abandoned by her listener (table 5.1).

Table 5.1   Listening styles

Speaker's gender	Listener's gender	Listener's style	Speaker's interpretation of listener
male	female	female	agreement
male	female	male	sterile and unfeminine
female	female	female	following the information
female	female	male	abandoned

There are other options available to women. Anita Roddick, for example, consciously chose a different approach in establishing and developing The Body Shop:

> A great advantage I had when I started The Body Shop was that I had never been to business school. As I didn't know how things were supposed to be done, I didn't know the rules and I didn't know the risks. As far as I was concerned there were no rules, and so I just went my own merry way working from gut instinct . . .
>
> We have too much respect for 'business' as perceived by 'businessmen'—which seems to mean just money, or the City, or banks . . . What you need (to run a business) is optimism, humanism, enthusiasm, intuition, curiosity, love, humour, magic and fun and that secret ingredient—euphoria. None of this appears on the curriculum of any business school.[6]

More and more, as women establish their own businesses, or achieve senior positions in existing organisations, they are choosing to bypass traditional male methods of managing and communicating and are using a 'feminine' style—a style that emphasises nurturing, compassion, open communication, empowerment, humour and enjoyment. And this is not a 'soft' option. It is a powerful business strategy which enables them to deal effectively with the most difficult situations.

Yet for many women neither adopting the male genderlect nor using a 'feminine' style are viable options. Up until now the majority of working women have chosen to remain in the traditional business system. They are mostly not in sufficiently senior positions to impose their own style on the organisation and yet strongly resist 'masculinising' their communication style.

So what options do these women have?

Deborah Tannen claims that if women and men understand each other's genderlects then it is possible to change if you choose to, or at least to improve relationships by accepting the differences.[7] We go further than this. We maintain that, in a business context, women will have to take the initiative. If we wish our voices to be heard (see figure 5.1) and listened to in the business world, there are a number of steps we need to take. Understanding the male genderlect is only the first of these steps.

Figure 5.1   In order for women to be heard

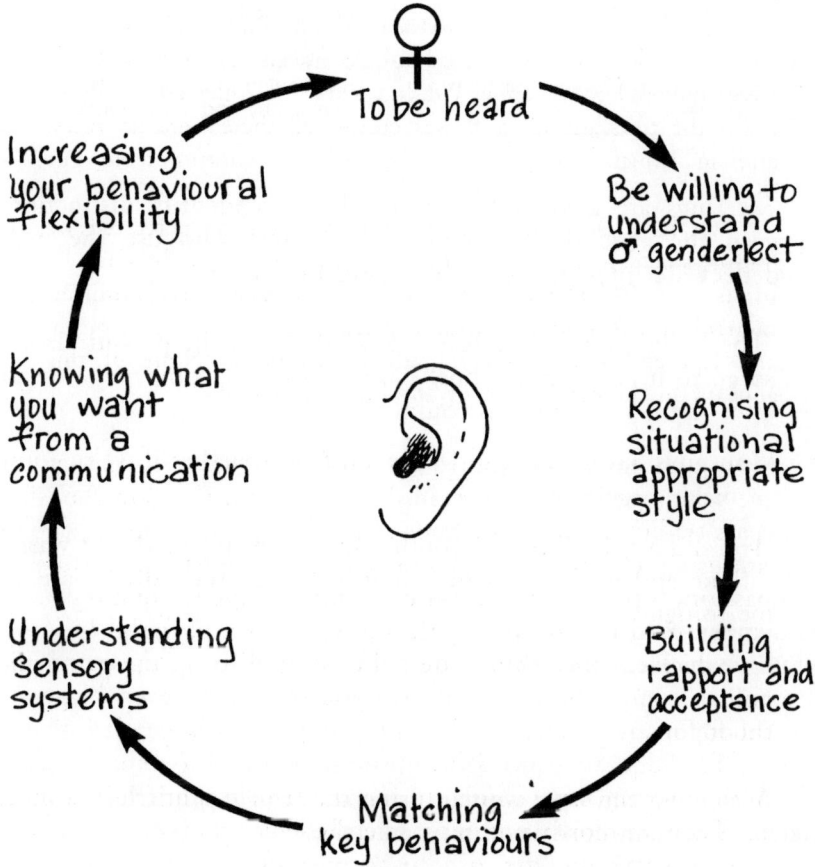

UNDERSTANDING THE MALE GENDERLECT

We have set out some of the key differences between the typical female and typical male communication patterns in table 5.2.[8]

Table 5.2 **Key differences between male and female communication patterns**

Male genderlect emphasises	Female genderlect emphasises
status	intimacy
independence	connection
hierarchy	minimising differences
giving instructions and orders	consensus; giving suggestions
arguing and interrupting	harmony; negotiating conflicts
elaborate systems of rules	encouraging participation
winners and losers	cooperation
protection	helping
silence	a talking/listening process
responding to problems with solutions and advice	responding to problems with empathy and understanding

Meetings are a great forum in which to identify distinctions between the genderlects. Those run by men who use the male genderlect are interspersed with phrases like these:

- 'The budget for the month is $125 000 and the pressure is on, so go to it and crucify those bastards from X company who are after the Global Bank account.'

- 'You guys have really got to get your act together if we're going to make target.'

- 'You did a great job last month. Now prove to me that it wasn't a fluke and do it again this month. By the way, drinks are on me tonight.'

- 'I've decided since things are going so well to up the game and hold a competition . . . to give you something even bigger to shoot for.'

A meeting run by a woman using the female genderlect is more likely to contain contain phrases like these:

- 'Our budget for this month is $125 000. We know it's going to be tough, so let's discuss how we go about achieving it.'

- 'Any suggestions as to what we can do about company X trying to get the Global Banking account from us?'

- 'We got a great result last month. Let's go out and celebrate!!'

- 'Things are going so well. As a team what do you think about the idea of some kind of incentive for over-achieving? I have some ideas but I'd also like to know what sort of incentive appeals to you.'

Football, one of the most sacred of male sports, is an example of how male values and the male genderlect is passed on. Young boys quickly learn to thread their way through the maze of rules, internalise the importance of their position in the hierarchy and that winning is everything, and start to use the accepted and acceptable masculine language. Phrases like 'Get the bastard', 'Flatten him', 'Beat the shit out of him', are equally applicable in football and in business.

Today, politics provides the most obvious example of the male ethic and male genderlect. The political arena is based on domination and control, centralising power in the hands of a few people, withholding information, conflict, an adversarial approach, a win/lose style and a hierarchical party structure. How do you feel as you listen to parliamentary debates, where politicians shout at each other, constantly interrupt and argue with each other and use 'denigration, ridicule and personal abuse'[9] as their preferred tactic?

The male genderlect is also what we are accustomed to in business. And in certain situations—for example, in a team of hard-hitting salesmen or truck drivers—it is useful for women to be able to use more male genderlect words and phrases. We are not suggesting here that women abandon their own genderlect in favour of the male genderlect, but that they learn to recognise the male genderlect and then make a choice about which genderlect is appropriate in a given situation. This increases their flexibility and choices of behaviour without sacrificing their natural style.

BUILDING RAPPORT AND ACCEPTANCE

Many of the finer distinctions we now have about communication are due to the work done by John Grinder and Richard Bandler.[10] By understanding concepts such as rapport building, matching behaviours and how we take in and use information (sensory systems), we begin to gain a deeper appreciation of our own and other people's communication processes. These skills apply across the board—not only to communicating with men, as is our emphasis here, but also to communicating with other women, other cultures and other generations.

We suggested in the previous section that women must be able to understand and use the male genderlect in appropriate situations. But this is not enough. Women must also be able to build rapport with, and gain acceptance from, their male colleagues at all levels.

What is rapport?

It is the ability to put yourself in someone else's shoes. When you are in rapport with another person you know it because the communication process, both verbal and non-verbal, flows easily. *You* feel comfortable, and so does the other person. It is an important ingredient in achieving your outcomes in any type of interaction, whether it is with a spouse, child, parent, friend, boss, colleague, subordinate or client.

We know when we don't have rapport with someone and the effect it has on our sense of wellbeing and our performance. If we don't have rapport with a colleague from another division of our organisation, we can say goodbye to being able to work together productively. And if we don't have rapport with our boss, our chances of getting the support we need for a new initiative are infinitesimal.

Just one note of warning before we proceed. According to Genie Laborde, there is one prerequisite for rapport.[11] It is *not* that you must like the person or people you are dealing with, but that you have trust in their competence for the task in which you are engaged. Without this trust it is just not possible to sustain rapport.

TRUST . . .

A MAJOR KEY
TO
RAPPORT

The following insights and techniques are offered for dealing with people with whom we do not find it easy to establish rapport, and who are important to our success or wellbeing (such as a difficult client or boss).

Matching behaviours

One technique that works particularly well in establishing rapport is matching another person's behaviour. There are two keys to this process:

- the ability to perceive fine distinctions in behaviour

- the flexibility to adapt some of these behaviours into your own communication style

Matching involves observing the person with whom you are communicating, selecting some of their behaviours and then exactly duplicating those behaviours. If they lean back in their chair, so do you. If they cross their legs, so do you. If they gesture a lot with their hands, so do you.

This enables you to step into the other person's world, see as they see, hear as they hear and feel as they feel.

As you can see from the mind map in figure 5.2,[12] many aspects of a person's behaviour can be matched—how they breathe, stand, sit, fold their arms, the pitch and tempo of their voice, any distinctive gestures they have. The most important of these factors is breathing. If a person is uncomfortable in a situation, their breathing will be erratic. Have you ever been conscious of holding your breath during a difficult telephone conversation? Michael Grinder actually equates rapport and breathing when he says, 'Rapport is to have the person breathing well'.[13]

It is important that matching is done respectfully. Michael Grinder has established some rules around this:[14]

- If you have the same cultural background, you can match up to 100 per cent of another person's voice, tone, pitch, speed and volume.

- You can match up to 75 per cent of facial expressions.

- 50 per cent of body posture can be matched.

- Up to 100 per cent of the other person's gestures can be matched when you are talking.

Figure 5.2   Matching

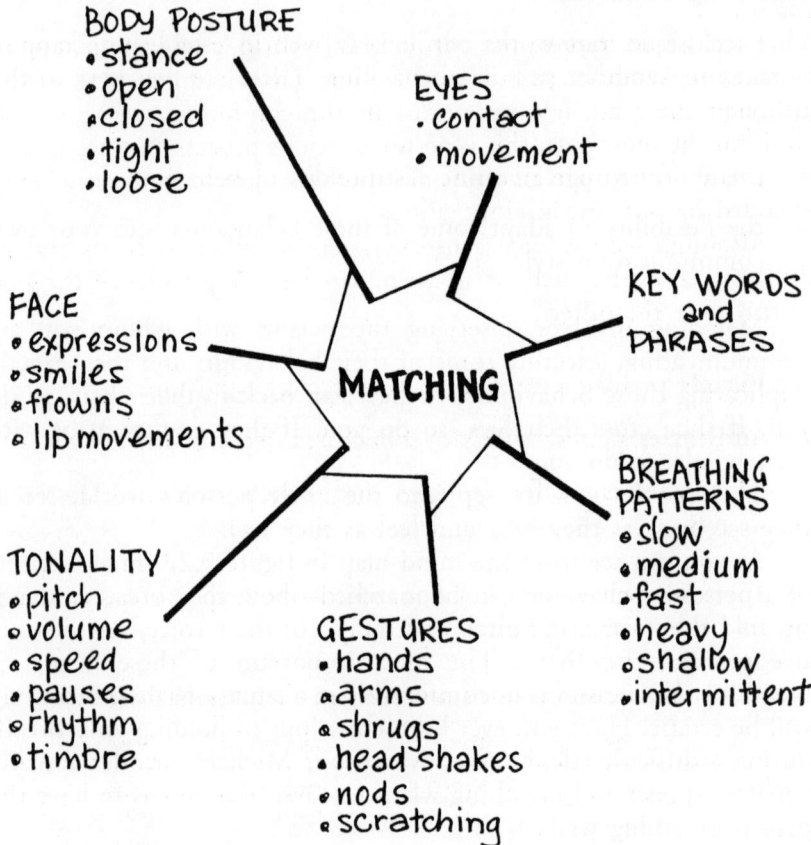

Matching is a natural, unconscious process. We do it all the time, intuitively, without realising it. Observe couples at a restaurant. When they have rapport, they tend to sit the same way, make similar gestures with their hands, laugh at the same time, and so on. If they are disagreeing or arguing, their body language tends to be dissimilar.

See the exercise at the end of the book on p. 193 to practise this skill.

Sensory systems

Another key to building rapport is understanding sensory systems or how we take in information and process it so that it has meaning for us.

Each of us represents our internal world and experiences in pictures or symbols, sounds and feelings (also in smells and tastes, although these are less important in the communication process). And, for the most part, this is an unconscious process. We are simply not aware of the huge amounts of inputs that are continuously being encoded by our unconscious minds.

Although we use each sensory system at different times and in different contexts, each of us seems to have a preference for one system over the others.

- **Visuals** prefer pictures to sounds, feelings and touch.

- **Auditories** prefer sounds over pictures, feelings and touch.

- **Kinaesthetics** prefer feelings and touch over pictures and sounds.

Table 5.3[15] gives some key behaviours that help in distinguishing visuals, auditories and kinaesthetics.

Table 5.3   How to distinguish visuals, auditories and kinaesthetics

	Eyes	Voice	Movement	Predicates
Visual		high, fast pace	body still, movement around eyes	focus look foggy hazy idea paint a picture
Auditory		tempo, medium pace	movement around mouth and ears	listen hear sound tune in loud and clear
Kinaesthetic		low, louder, slow pace	lots of movement from neck down	feel handle catch get the drift pain in the neck

You can identify whether the person to whom you are talking prefers the visual, auditory or kinaesthetic mode by listening to their language, watching their eye movements and observing their breathing and voice patterns.

But what about you? Do you know which is your preferred sensory system? Table 5.3 should give you some clues and, for confirmation, try the simple questionnaire on 'What is your preferred sensory system?' at the end of the book (p. 193).

It is important to note that we do not use one sense exclusively—few of us are purely visual, purely auditory or purely kinaesthetic. However, most of us have a preferred way of taking in information and representing it internally, and this is what we need to observe in our communication with others.

'. . . people do not use one sense exclusively,
and you will only limit yourself
if you categorise people in this way.'
Genie Laborde[16]

Tina has a strong preference for her auditory channel. She has a melodious voice, and an uncanny ability to pick up accents and languages. She processes information through dialogue inside her head, and often appears to be off in another world while she is doing this. She can remember whole conversations, and can often repeat them almost word for word.

Tim's preferred sensory system is kinaesthetic. He likes to make physical contact with people as he is talking and often stands close to them. He learns most readily when he is able to experience or practise something, and loves physical activities of all kinds.

Research on teachers in the United States has shown that:[17]

up to 60%	prefer	visual	as their primary input channel
10–15%	prefer	auditory	
over 30%	prefer	kinaesthetic	

While teachers do not represent the whole population, there does seem to be a natural chronological progression from kinaesthetic through auditory to visual for most people. In other words, most five-year-olds will use the kinaesthetic mode as their primary input channel, teenagers tend to be strongly auditory, while the typical adult prefers the visual mode.

Some more clues to help you distinguish a person's preferred input channel:

Visuals

Visuals will use expressions like:

I get the picture	*the future looks hazy to me*
get a perspective on . . .	*in light of*
beyond a shadow of a doubt	*tunnel vision*
well defined	*clear cut*

Their eyes will move up or become unfocused when they access information.

Their voices are more highly pitched, and their breathing is more shallow and higher in their chests than in those who prefer the auditory and kinaesthetic modes.

Auditories

Auditories use phrases like:

that sounds right	*just listen to me*
clear as a bell	*describe in detail*
pay attention to . . .	*voice an opinion*
give an account of . . .	*state your purpose*
afterthought	*enquire into . . .*

Their eyes will move sideways to the left or right when accessing information.

Their breathing is even and comes from the mid-chest region, and their voices have a rhythmical tempo.

Kinaesthetics

Kinaesthetics will typically say:

that feels right	*I find it hard to grasp*
boils down to . . .	*smooth operator*
hand in hand	*heated argument*
sharp as a tack	*slipped my mind*
stiff upper lip	*start from scratch*

Their eyes will move downwards when they access information.
They tend to breathe from their stomach and they speak more slowly and with a more deeply pitched voice than visuals or auditories.

Given this information, what can you do with it, both inside and outside the business context?

- Increase your own flexibility.

For example, if you are comfortable with the visual and kinaesthetic modes, practise the auditory mode. Set yourself the task of observing an auditory person and then, using your observations as a role model, be an auditory for one whole day—talking, breathing and accessing information as an auditory. Once you can talk readily in each of the sensory systems, you will find that you understand others more easily.

- Use the preferred sensory system of the person with whom you are communicating.

We all feel more comfortable with someone who is communicating with us through our preferred sensory system, as our unconscious mind doesn't have to translate the messages. As long as you are reading the other person's primary input channel correctly, you will find that it is easier to establish rapport and that you can influence them more readily.

- If you are talking to a group of people, or addressing a meeting, use language from each of the sensory systems. That way you will make sure that you get through to everyone at least some of the time.

Some of the benefits you can gain from this knowledge are:

- a greater understanding of others, including men, by entering their world

- an ability to influence others and to be seen as a person of influence

- consistently reaching your desired communication outcomes

- achieving long-term mutually beneficial relationships in business

KNOWING WHAT YOU WANT FROM A COMMUNICATION

The next step is to be as precise as possible about the purpose of a communication.

In business, unless you have a reason, there is very little point in taking the trouble to understand the other person's sensory system and develop rapport. So decide the outcome or result that you want from a communication, and try to make this outcome as specific as possible. Use sensory data to help you clarify this process.

> ### *COMMUNICATION*
> ### *IS THE RESPONSE*
> ### *YOU GET*[18]

When you have your outcome what will you

see   ?

hear   ?

feel   ?

Maria's story . . .

Maria wanted to get agreement from her general manager on next year's budget for her department. After she had completed her budget estimates and before she went into the meeting with the GM, she imagined what she would see, hear and feel at the end of the meeting:

- She could see herself coming out of the GM's office at the end of the meeting with her budget spreadsheet approved and signed off in the GM's distinctive handwriting.

- Inside her head she heard the GM congratulating her on her attention to detail and her clearly expressed annual forecasts.

- She could feel the smile on her face after the GM's positive words and the internal glow that comes from knowing you have done a good job.

In top level international sport there is often little difference in ability between athletes. Mental attitude can make that critical difference in performance. If you can see, hear and feel yourself winning a race, or sinking a crucial putt, or winning the vital game, then you have a powerful edge over an athlete who has no clear image of future success.

Roma's story . . .

As champion swimmer of Kenya, the main difference between me and the other competitors was that I expected to win. Before every race, I imagined myself getting to the finishing line before the others. In the short races, the imagined gap between me and the other competitors was quite short, but in the long races I always saw myself several body lengths, if not pool lengths, ahead of them.

Before and during the race, I always felt a familiar and exhilarating rush of adrenalin which gave me a feeling of confidence. This was reinforced by hearing the crowd barracking—to me, they were always shouting for me to win.

Similarly for women in business. If you have a clear idea of what it will be like when you have achieved your outcome—what it will feel like, what you will be hearing and what you will be seeing—then it is easier to turn your imagined future into reality. This is really an extension of believing in yourself.

Let's say your outcome is to successfully negotiate a contract. To make your outcome a reality, try the following steps:

- believe you can do it

- visualise yourself doing it

- think backwards from the future to the present to work out the steps you need to take

- go and do it!

INCREASING YOUR BEHAVIOURAL FLEXIBILITY

If you have followed all the above steps and the way you are communicating with a particular person is not getting you the outcomes that you want, then you need to change your behaviour.

> *IF WHAT YOU ARE DOING*
> *IS NOT WORKING . . .*
>
> *DO SOMETHING DIFFERENT*

This is not necessarily easy to do. Old behaviours are familiar, comfortable and feel like 'us', even when they are not giving us the results we want. Family and friends may feel uncomfortable if we adopt new behaviours. And trying a new behaviour is a risk.

The point is . . . how badly do you want to achieve your outcome? Are you willing to do something different and to increase the range of behaviours available to you?

You can increase your behavioural flexibility by:

- being precise about the outcome you want to get

- being aware of your existing behaviour and communication pattern with a particular person

- noticing what is and what isn't working for you

- becoming aware of other possible communication and behaviour patterns by observing and role modelling other people[19]

- being willing to try some of these other behaviours

- knowing that a different behaviour will get you a different response, and being willing to keep changing until you get the response you want

> *'In a given situation, all things being equal, the person with the greatest requisite variety influences the most.'*
> Michael Grinder[20]

The best way to achieve flexibility is to practise. Do some different things, or do some things differently. For example:

- pretend you are 5 years old again for a day

- do or learn a new activity—anything you haven't done before, from hang-gliding to knitting to going to the ballet to watching the sun rise

- go to work a different way

- change your typical behaviour in a meeting. For example, if you are normally quiet then contribute a lot; if you are normally the leader become one of the group

• imagine that you are the chief executive officer of a multi-national organisation for a day

• consciously choose to be a male colleague that you know. Put yourself in his shoes. What does it feel like?

Kerry's story . . .

I have a twenty-year-old son. When he was younger, and I was irritated at one of his behaviours (e.g. leaving a mess of dishes in the kitchen) he would justify himself aggressively. After the encounter we would both feel angry and frustrated.

I have noticed recently that he has changed his response. When I am angry with him, he now agrees with me that the behaviour I am angry about is undesirable and that he should do something about it. This defuses my anger and we can then carry on with an amicable discussion (although he still leaves dirty dishes in the kitchen).

He has learnt flexibility to achieve the outcome he wants from the interaction, which is to keep the peace between us. I still have to figure out how I need to change to achieve the outcome I want, which is to have him take responsibility for his own dishes!!

IN SUMMARY

Despite the changes occurring in business structures and values, women in the business world are still essentially operating in foreign territory. The 'game' is male, the rules are male, the communication process is male, the language is male. In order to fit comfortably into this world, women need to be able to understand how men view the business world and how they communicate with each other. They need this understanding not to become male clones, but in order to develop rapport with men and flexibility in their communication style.

The first step in communicating in the corporate environment is understanding the male communication process—the male 'genderlect', as Deborah Tannen calls it. But this is only the first step. In order to be able to choose the most effective communication patterns to use, women need finer distinctions about communication. These distinctions include the ability to develop rapport—using skills such as understanding and matching sensory systems.

Once we understand these distinctions, we are better able to see things from the other person's perspective and are more able to develop behavioural flexibility. And behavioural flexibility is the key. As long as we know the outcome we want from a communication, we can adjust our communication and behaviour patterns until we achieve this outcome. This way it is possible for women to adapt their style to the situation without sacrificing their own preferred style.

Philippa Bond is a trainer and business consultant. Her approach to clients incorporates the communication skills we have been discussing.

As a trainer promoting my own programs in corporate environments I find that I come up against some attitudes and approaches that are not really as open or welcoming as they could be. I understand that it is my responsibility to sell the benefits of such programs to training managers or employers within organisations. However, it does seem that sometimes I enter into negotiations 'behind the eight ball' because I do not come in the package of a classic business man who so many training managers and organisations are familiar dealing with. Because of this I have found the skills of rapport building to be invaluable. They should be in the briefcase of every business person.

I was invited in for an interview to discuss a training for executive management for a large banking corporation. I had been dealing with the training manager by telephone and so we had spoken prior to our meeting, which eased my anxiety to some degree. My main reason for having this meeting was to sell a training I was promoting and to then develop an ongoing relationship which would secure further trainings. I knew that this would only happen if I could get on well with this training manager. I knew if he liked my presentation style and product and felt at ease with me then an ongoing relationship could be possible.

So a deep breath . . . here goes. I can remember so clearly my first thought when I saw him: 'Thank goodness he is short too!' This I thought was a good start. At least we had that in common! I did not think, however, that it would have been a useful start to draw attention to this fact and start the conversation with something like 'Good morning short stuff!'. With a polite greeting we sat down and began our conversation.

He positioned himself opposite me across a large desk so I gracefully moved my chair to the side of the desk, indicating that I was wanting to share some information with him. This caused him to turn his chair so he was not sitting square on to the desk, like me. The similarities were building.

I noticed that he had a low vocal tone when he spoke and he spoke slowly, taking deep inhalations between thoughts. I slowed my speech and dropped my tone, even though this was not my natural style and difficult to do given the sensations and feelings of nervousness in my body. I also paid special attention to my breathing so that we were breathing at a similar rate.

Most of the interview was taken up with me pacing this man and building rapport in such a way that we could talk on the same level and understand each other. The more I paced him the more I seemed to get an understanding of what he was wanting and what his concerns were. This was valuable information when it came to presenting the training and supporting documentation because I was then able to tailor the presentation to his needs and concerns. If I had not spent time paying attention to him and where he was coming from I quite feasibly could have missed these valuable clues.

When I realised that he was getting excited about the training I was presenting I recognised that it was now my time for leading. I brought out my trump cards; time to seal the deal and close the sale—to lead him in the direction that I intended for the interview. Because I had an outcome and intention before entering into this negotiation I had somewhere to lead him. If I had just gone into the negotiation waiting to see what happened then it is difficult to lead anywhere, because anywhere we ended up would have been fine.

As I walked away from his office, with a warm glow inside, after getting a verbal agreement with written confirmation to follow, I started to think, 'Am I selling myself out becoming like him just to sell this training? Where was the real "me" in this interaction?' I thought deeply about what it means to be in business and to be a part of negotiations. I believe that the training I present will definitely be of benefit to the individuals and also to the organisation. It is definitely of benefit to me to get more work so I can continue my business and continue adding to the professional and personal development of business people. Therefore, I concluded after much thought, given such an integral outcome then I was still being true to myself in such interactions. It is when I do not have a reason for building rapport that I could lose myself in pacing someone else to nowhere.

My relationship with this training manager continues on a very professional basis. We enjoy our conversations when we talk and we continue to do business. It is wonderful doing business with friends![21]

The issue that Philippa debates with herself after her negotiating process—that of her integrity and whether she is being true to herself when she is using the skills of rapport building—is one that women have been facing ever since they entered the male-dominated business world. In the past, women have felt that their choices have been between adopting the male style or remaining true to their own natural style. We now have more choices, and thus more flexibility, about our communication style. By matching our communication style to the person and the situation we can achieve good long-term working relationships as well as our immediate outcomes.

And just as women's innate communication processes have been misunderstood and undervalued in the business world, so also are our natural approaches to decision making. Women have an innate decision making ability that is not often validated or recognised in the business world . . .

6

DOING IT DIFFERENTLY . . .[1]

'One of the biggest fears that keeps us from moving ahead
with our lives is our difficulty in making decisions . . . The
irony, of course, is that by not choosing, we *are* choosing.'

Susan Jeffers[2]

. . . HOW WE MAKE DECISIONS

We all make decisions—dozens of them—every day. Some are big
and some small; some have immediate consequences and some
long-term consequences; some are personal and some are work-
related. Just getting out of bed requires a decision making process,
as does deciding what to have for breakfast, what clothes to wear,
driving the car, answering the phone, having a coffee break, and so
on through each day. Even procrastination is a decision!

The interesting thing is that each of us, often without being
consciously aware of it, has a fully developed system for making
decisions. We mostly could not say how we actually make decisions.
It's often not until something goes wrong or we're faced with a
decision that has serious consequences that we consciously feel the
need to stop and think about the choices we have.

Why is decision making important?

Simply this:

> *YOU*
> *CAN NOT*
> *NOT*
> ***MAKE DECISIONS***

In this sense, not making a decision is really a decision to allow ourselves to be controlled by others or by our environment. This may be okay for decisions such as what to have for dinner or what film to go and see. But is it okay for decisions at work, or decisions about our careers or our lives? This is particularly important for women to consider. All too often in the past important decisions affecting women's lives have been made by others. The patriarchy dictated that women should obey. Women grew up obeying their fathers, transferred this obedience to their husbands (in the Western marriage ceremony women have traditionally promised to 'love, honour and obey' their husbands), and readily carried this pattern into the workplace.

We all make decisions in a number of ways, depending on

- their purpose
- whether they are
  - routine decisions
  - short-term decisions
  - long-term decisions

- our own internal decision making mechanism

If we want to improve our ability to make decisions, it is helpful if we first understand what drives our internal decision making mechanism. Anthony Robbins claims that there are five key components:[3]

- **Our strongest beliefs** and the unconscious rules we set up for ourselves. These determine whether we make decisions that empower us or limit us.

- **Our values**, which determine our sense of right and wrong, good and bad, appropriateness and inappropriateness. It is through our values that we judge decisions, both our own and those of others.

- **Our memories and experiences.** No matter whether our experiences are good or bad, memories will be associated with them. With more memories and experiences, we have a bigger and more varied choice bank. This means that we are not locked into one, or only a few ways, of choosing to make a decision.

- **The habitual questions we ask ourselves**. We all carry out a continuous internal dialogue with ourselves—for example, as you are reading this chapter, your self-talk is asking you whether or not you agree with what we have written. And this self-talk is influenced by your outlook on life. Some of us view the world optimistically and have positive expectations. Others have pessimistic expectations and tend to think that any actions we take will be futile.[4] The internal questions we unconsciously ask ourselves reflect this and in turn influence the decisions we make.

- **Our state** when we make a decision—for example, when we are feeling angry, we will make a different decision from when we are feeling excited, sad or calm.

The synergistic interaction of these driving forces provides the fuel for the engine which drives us to make certain decisions. The good news is that by being aware of these factors we can consciously decide to change our decision making process.

Left brain/right brain

One other factor is critically important and yet relatively unexplored in our decision making process, and that is how we use our brain.

Since the work of Roger Sperry and Robert Ornstein in the late 1960s and early 1970s,[5] we have known that the two hemispheres of our brains perform different functions and are linked by a network of fibres called the corpus collosum. For most people the left hemisphere deals with logic, numbers, language, reasoning, analysis and sequence. The right hemisphere influences colour, rhythm, imagination, space and spontaneity.

Do you know which is your dominant hemisphere? Do you prefer left or right brain activities? Try the 'Brain dominance questionnaire' at the end of this book (see page 197) and confirm what you already intuitively know about your brain preference.

Robert Ornstein also found that specialisation tends to develop one side of the brain only and that when the lesser used side is stimulated the result is a great increase in effectiveness. What this means in practice is that when we use both hemispheres we become far more effective than if we predominantly use only one hemisphere of our brain.

Table 6.1 Key characteristics of the left and right hemispheres

Left hemisphere	Right hemisphere
sequencing	random
logic	intuition
fact	creativity, imagination
words, numbers	rhythm, music
black and white	colour
small picture	big picture
detail, parts	whole
reality-based	fantasy-oriented
time	space
analysis	synthesis
thinking	feelings, emotions
language, reading	shapes, patterns
verbal	non-verbal
symbols	concrete
listening	visualisation

Since the Industrial Revolution in particular, there has been a strong emphasis in Western cultures on developing the left brain. School syllabuses and the education process emphasise the 'three Rs'—conformity, regulation and discipline. The work environment stresses punctuality, hierarchy, job descriptions and standardised procedures.

> *'Mass education was*
> *the ingenious machine*
> *constructed by industrialism*
> *to produce the kind of adults it needed.'*
> Alvin Toffler[6]

The emphasis on the left brain served the needs of the industrial age well. But we are no longer in the industrial age. As we saw in chapter 2, we are now into the information age. And with the waves of change caused by the rapid expansion of technology, our needs are changing, while our education systems and our work values are still locked into the time warp of the industrial era.

Part of our success in dealing with continuing accelerating change will be our ability to make decisions and to modify our values, beliefs and attitudes. The strengths of the right brain come into their own here. It is with the right brain that we can deal with new and changing situations, generate spontaneous and creative alternatives and look at possibilities with a global perspective. Our long-term dependence on the left brain abilities of logic, analysis and sequence will become a liability unless we lose some of our reverence for its functions, and transfer this reverence, not only to the right brain, but to a validation and celebration of the vital role of the whole brain.

The value that Western culture traditionally places on left brain thinking is a direct result of the patriarchal system and predominant male values. Talking about the United States, Warren Bennis says that 'organisational life is a left-brain culture, meaning logical, analytical, technical, controlled, conservative and administrative. We, to the extent we are its products, are dominated and shaped by those same characteristics'.[7] These comments can be extended to Western organisations in general. In particular, the business tool of decision making has been regarded by management theorists as a logical, sequential, unemotional left brain process.

Eastern cultures have recognised for a long time the importance of complementary forms. It is from the East that we get the concept of yin and yang[8] and that one does not exist without the other. They are in fact both part of the whole, just as the left hemisphere and the right hemisphere make up the whole brain. In the West we are also starting to recognise that there needs to be a shift: as a culture and as individuals we need to encourage more right brain qualities. It is the intuitive, creative and 'big picture' focus of the right brain that will help us to cope with the enormous changes escalating all around us.

In the same way there is more than logical thinking involved in effective decision making. The right brain, with its ability to think laterally, creatively, spontaneously, wholistically and randomly, also has an important role to play in decision making. So also do previously ill-defined senses such as 'gut feel', intuition and knowing, that also come from the right brain. Every good salesperson knows that people buy with emotion and justify with logic!

> *'Most managerial decisions are not based solely on a systematic and logical process of data gathering, but also on an intuitive sense of what will work. This sense comes from the knowing part of ourselves, which we need to learn to trust.'*
> Natasha Josefowitz[9]

And women have a clear advantage here over men. Although we have all been through the same education process, women are less entrenched in the left brain culture than men. We are 'allowed' to show more emotion and we are, in general, more comfortable in the right hemisphere areas of intuition, feelings and 'big picture' thinking.

What we will do now is develop some alternative ways of making decisions in order to give you finer distinctions and more choice in the process.

ROUTINE DECISION MAKING

We are continually making routine decisions (figure 6.1), and we often don't even recognise this as a decision making process. What happens is that the brain recognises a familiar pattern and automatically makes and implements a decision—in the same way that a similar problem or situation has always been resolved before.

Examples of routine decision making include:

- filing, where the brain responds automatically and unconsciously as long as it recognises a familiar pattern

- entering routine data into accounts ledgers

- many daily chores both at work and home, such as showering, dressing, driving a car, answering a phone, taking coffee breaks

- routinely signing your name to letters or cheques without consciously looking at what you are signing

When a change occurs, you will often notice people doing what they used to do out of routine—unconscious decision making. For example, in our office the reception area has recently been moved. The old reception area is now open floor space and yet people are still walking around a non-existent reception desk!

'I rely on my brain
. . . to come to the right decision for me.'
Hans Eysenck[10]

Figure 6.1   Routine decision making

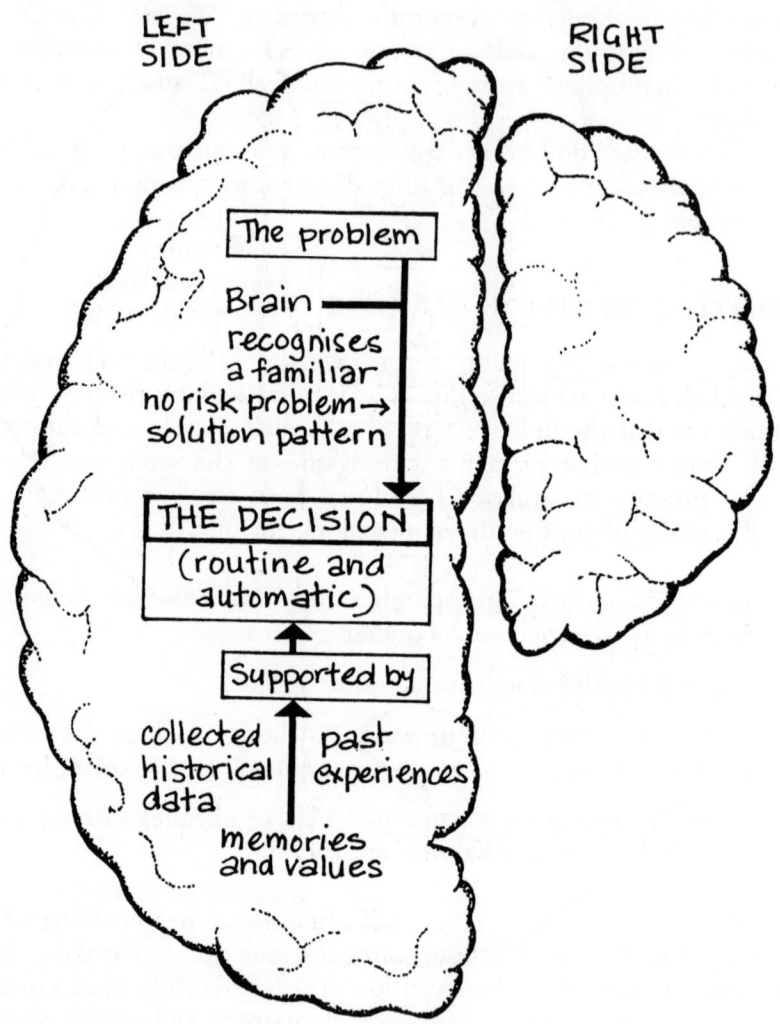

Routine decision making saves us from going into overload and conserves our mental energy for non-routine and more important decisions. And this is valuable, as long as we recognise that it is an automatic process, and stop occasionally to question the decisions we are making.

Figure 6.2 Left brain decision making

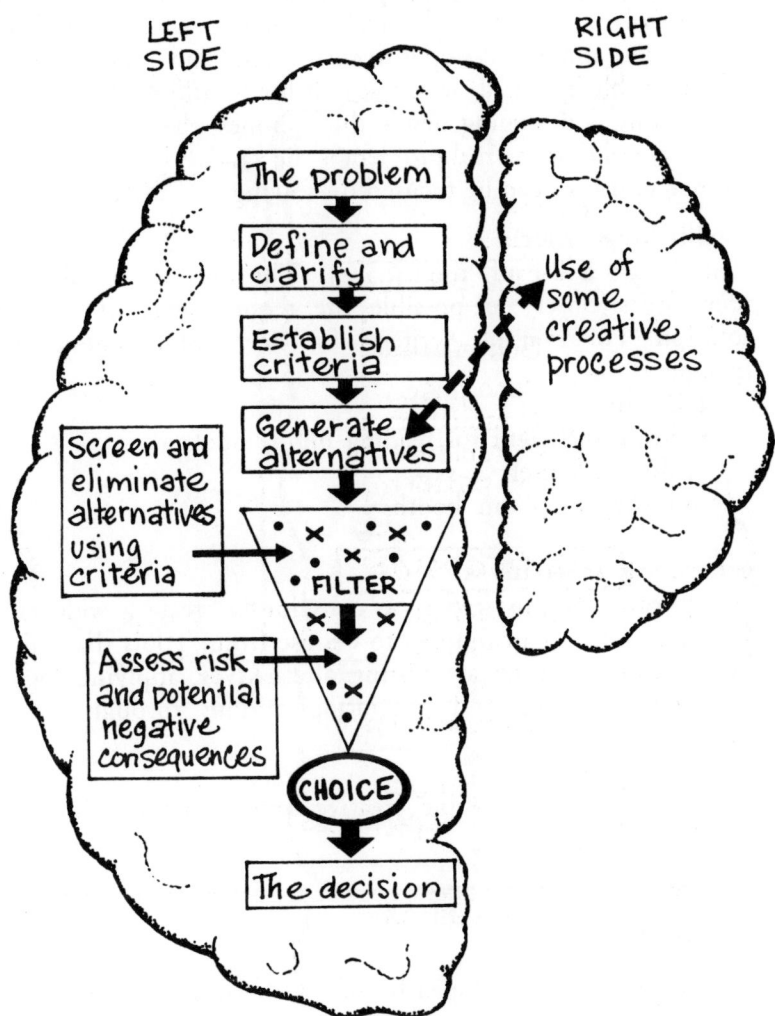

LEFT BRAIN DECISION MAKING

Left brain decision making (figure 6.2), or close relations of this process, are to be found in most classical management texts.

According to this process, decision making is a series of sequential, logical steps, as follows:

- **defining and clarifying the problem**
  This involves identifying the 'real' problem—what it is and what it isn't. The aim of this step is to ensure a full and clear description of the problem to help in the search for solutions. For example, if the issue is designing new public phones, then a clarification might reveal that the real problem is the vandalism of the phones, so that solutions can be focused on solving the vandalising.

- **establishing criteria**
  Criteria are a list of 'must haves'. The purpose of this is to identify as closely as possible the requirements of the final solution. For example, criteria for new public phones may include:
  > indestructibility
  > lighting sufficient for reading phone books
  > visibility of user
  > sound-proof phone booths

- **generating alternatives**
  The purpose of this step is to consciously create a wide range and large number of options to choose from. Tools that can be used include looking at existing alternatives, applying logical, left brain thinking and generating options through creative techniques.

Two of the many possible creative options are brainstorming and synectics.[11]

Brainstorming

Brainstorming was developed by Alex Osborn in 1957. It is a group activity for generating ideas and there are certain rules that apply:

- suspend criticism and judgment

- write ideas on a flip chart or whiteboard

- generate as many ideas as possible, the wilder the better

- set a time limit for each brainstorm

Synectics

Synectics was developed by William J. Gordon in the 1960s. It aims to generate one new idea to solve a problem. A group leader organises and runs the session on behalf of a client who has the problem. A climate that discourages criticism and encourages creative thinking is created.

There are six stages to the process:

- *A brief statement of the problem*
  The client gives the group a time-constrained overview of the problem. For example, the problem may be the phone booths mentioned above.

- *Goal wishes*
  The group identifies 'must haves' in the form of 'wishes'. The client then selects the wish that is most attractive to them. For example, in the case of the phone booth, the client may select the wish of indestructibility for the group to focus on.

- *An excursion*
  This is used to generate new ideas. The group is asked to look at something that is totally different from the actual problem. For example, they may be asked to come up with ideas about indestructibility in connection with a holiday or a desert or a relationship or writing a book.

- *Force fit*
  The group forces their excursion ideas on to the problem of phone booths.

- *Itemised response*
  Here, the group looks at the benefits as well as problems and concerns around the suggested solutions.

- *Possible solution*
  The client selects their favoured option.

- **screening and eliminating alternatives**
  This step involves comparing each alternative against the criteria and against other important factors like the goals and resources of the organisation. The purpose is to eliminate all alternatives except those which give a close fit.

- **assessing the risk and potential negative consequences**
  The purpose here is to thoroughly examine the alternatives that have passed the screen in order to identify weak points and carefully test seemingly attractive alternatives.

- **making a choice**
  The closest options are compared and the alternative that is an acceptable risk and that offers a close fit with the criteria is chosen.

This approach to decision making relies mostly on the left brain. It is only when creative techniques such as synectics and brainstorming are used that some right brain activities are involved.

Left brain processing is the basis of mathematical and computer models of decision making. When there are many variables to be considered, it is a useful way to reduce them to manageable proportions. However, it is not the only or the most effective way to generate alternatives or to make a final decision. For men, just as much as for women, it is like operating with one hand (or half of your brain!) tied behind your back.

Despite the rhetoric in text books, there is little evidence that left brain decision making really is the way that most business decisions are made, and even less evidence that it is a favoured process for personal decision making.

RIGHT BRAIN DECISION MAKING

In right brain decision making (figure 6.3) the essence of the process is that a decision is made at a 'gut' level and then justified, if necessary, by facts and figures. (And remember that statistics can be made to tell us anything we want to hear.)

In this process, the decision often occurs spontaneously, and is the result of:

- previously accumulated knowledge and data

- experiences and memories

- values

- beliefs and attitudes

- intuition, 'gut feel' and knowing

Figure 6.3 Right brain decision making

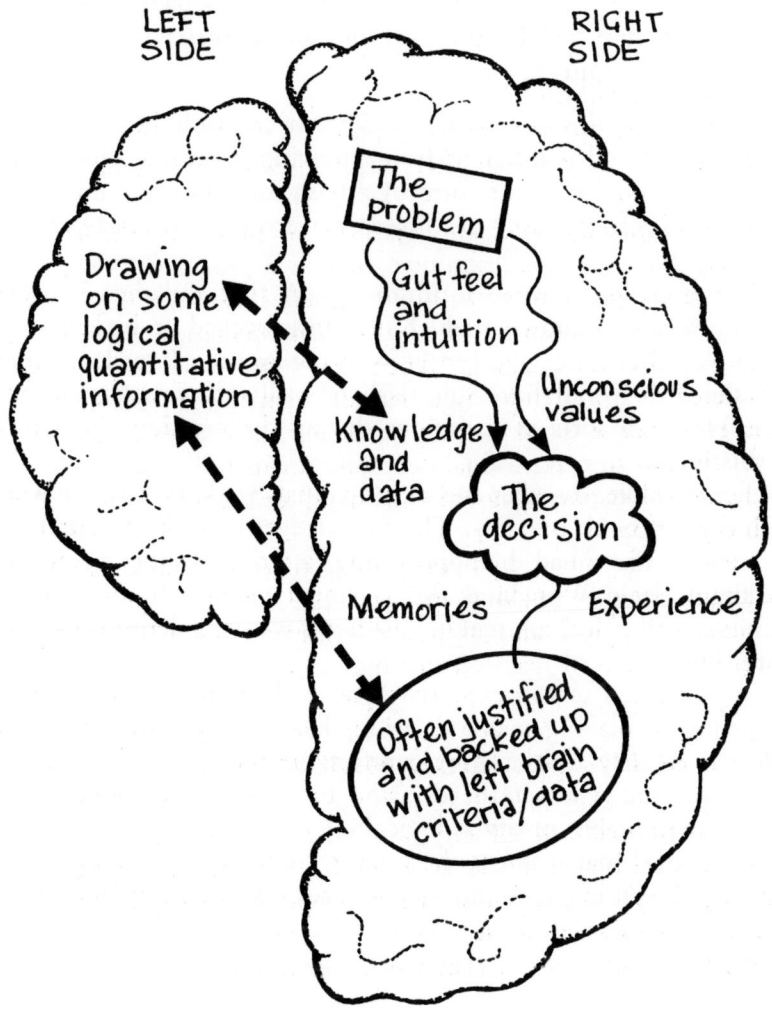

Intuition and *knowing* are very different from *knowledge*:

Knowledge is associated with left brain data, proof and criteria. It relies on the known, almost as if it can be calculated. It is quantifiable.

Knowing is not logical or based on hard core fact. It is associated with a deep inner certainty that feels right. If you want to dismiss or ignore it you can't because it remains as a nagging feeling in the gut. It is beyond the provable, until what you know (your gut feel) manifests.

Intuition is also not based on logic. It can only be proven after the event and is different from knowing because it comes to us instantaneously in the form of a flash, or a hunch, and because of this it can be easily dismissed or overridden by left brain data.

There are times when intuition occurs first and then is backed up with a certain knowing which in turn is backed up by knowledge (fact). At other times you can be working away in knowledge mode and suddenly you'll have this flash of brilliance or creativity. We experienced all sorts of variations during the creation and writing of this book.

For example, together and as individuals we knew that we would both write a book one day. The knowledge, or subject matter, was not clear until we had the opportunity to write a trainer's guide and workbook for a Women & Management video.[12] In this chapter, the idea for the decision making diagrams was very definitely a 'flash' (intuition).

If you listen to top executives you will often hear them openly admitting to making major decisions based on gut feel. The more experienced they are the more comfortable they are with instinctive decisions. And whether the decision turns out to be good or bad they can inevitably justify it logically.

At middle management the picture changes. Decisions based on gut feel are still made but are not so readily accepted by more senior managers.

Roma's story . . .

Instantaneously I decided that my team must know. Then I was 'told' not to say anything until my replacement had been found. I agreed, even though this went against my normal people management style and what I intuitively knew was right.

My fears were realised a few days later when an internal appointment was made. Through the grapevine my team learned that I was moving to another role and that someone else was going to be their manager.

Based on our relationship in the past I knew that they would have preferred hearing the news from me first and that way I could have reassured them that the proposed changes would work out okay for all of us. So, as soon as one of them came to me and said that they'd heard rumours, I met with all of them and apologised. They told me that none of them could understand my inconsistency and why I hadn't said something in the first place.

What I learned from this experience is—no matter who wants to persuade me to decide differently, in future I will trust what I intuitively know is the better decision at the time.

The evidence to date, which is largely based on observation and discussion, is that gut feel, intuition, knowing and right brain thinking tend to come easily and naturally to most women. As more and more women reach levels of power and influence, this difference in approach will be recognised as valuable. It will be reinforced as organisations increasingly change in the direction of greater flexibility and creativity. As a result, this type of decision making will become more common and more accepted.

There is something to watch out for with decisions made in this way. And that is that you may tend to be unconsciously biased. It's a bit like automatic decision making. If it's your preferred way of making decisions then you may not always consider other options simply because you don't stop to think about it.

WHOLE BRAIN DECISION MAKING

Whole brain decision making (figure 6.4) is another example of how we can value differences. If we want to look at the big picture, if we want to generate ideas and new approaches, we need to put the right brain into motion. The left brain helps us to choose ideas and

Figure 6.4 Whole brain decision making

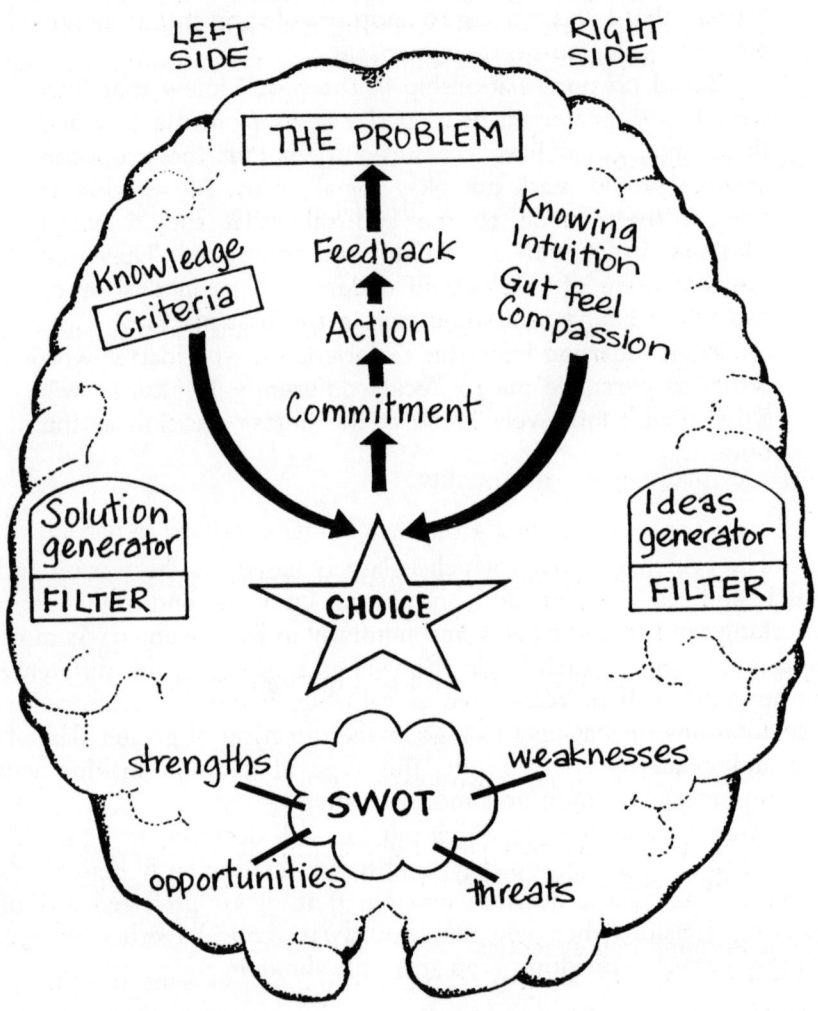

define the details. What we get by putting the right brain together with the left brain is a whole range of other possibilities—the effect is synergistic. The sum of the parts is greater than the whole.

With this type of decision making the key is *flexibility*. More options are available to us, and we can consider things from a wholistic point of view. There are no constraints, no set ways in which to proceed.

Even though it might be very underutilised, all of us have a right brain. The exercise on 'Accessing the right brain' at the end of the book (see p. 200) gives some strategies for accessing and using it.

Ideas generator

Here are some useful hints for ideas generation:

- Choose to be in a right brain state.

- Keep the ideas coming, no matter how insignificant or irrelevant they may seem.

- Keep it light-hearted, fun and humorous.

- Go for quantity, not quality.

- If you are doing it in a group, encourage everyone to participate.

- Create a safe environment so that no idea is considered 'dumb'.

- Consciously choose not to criticise or judge.

- Use colour and a whiteboard or flip chart paper.

- Choose one person to be the scribe.

- Trust that the process works.

Some techniques that your right brain will enjoy and that are extremely useful ways of generating ideas are listed below:

Brainstorming and synectics
We have already looked at brainstorming and synectics in the context of left brain decision making. Even though they are right brain processes they can be made even more 'right brained' and enjoyable if you follow the guidelines we have suggested above.

Lateral word association
A word is chosen randomly—for example, from a dictionary or any other book. Associations between this word and the decision to be made are teased out and written down.

Post-it™ notes game

This is similar to word association. Write down whatever words associated with the decision to be made come into your mind. Using coloured pens or textas, write as many words as you can using one Post-it™ for each word.

After the writing session, the Post-its™ are stuck on to a wall or a large piece of cardboard, sorted into categories, and condensed, reduced and refined. This part of the process becomes increasingly left brained, although it is important to allow for new ideas (new Post-its™) to be added.

We used Post-its™ as the initial ideas generator for this book. It helped us to sort out the main ideas that we needed to cover and gave us our first pass at chapter headings.

Mind mapping[13]

Mind maps (figure 6.5) are a right brain way of taking notes, planning, preparing a presentation or a report, memorising, learning and generating ideas. The technique was originally developed by Tony Buzan as an alternative to the traditional style of note taking that we all learned at school.

We were taught to take notes in a linear form, line after line, from left to right, from top to bottom and in black (or blue) on white. This is a very left brain approach!

We now know that the brain remembers things that are memorable, interesting, unusual and colourful. So in mind mapping, the purpose is to create a striking visual record of our ideas, or thoughts, or study sessions, or summaries of books, or lectures, or presentations, or whatever.

The subject heading is written somewhere on the page—often in the middle—and circled or made to stand out. Then key words, ideas and associations branch out from this. Use colour, pictures, symbols—anything that makes it memorable and fun for you.

Mind maps were the second stage of ideas generation for this book. We developed mind maps for each chapter, for our desired format and layout and for the publishing process.

SWOT

We need a process for looking at the ideas we have generated. SWOT acts as a filter, and is also a way of generating further ideas.

Take each of the ideas that have been generated, and one by

Figure 6.5   Mind map of mind mapping

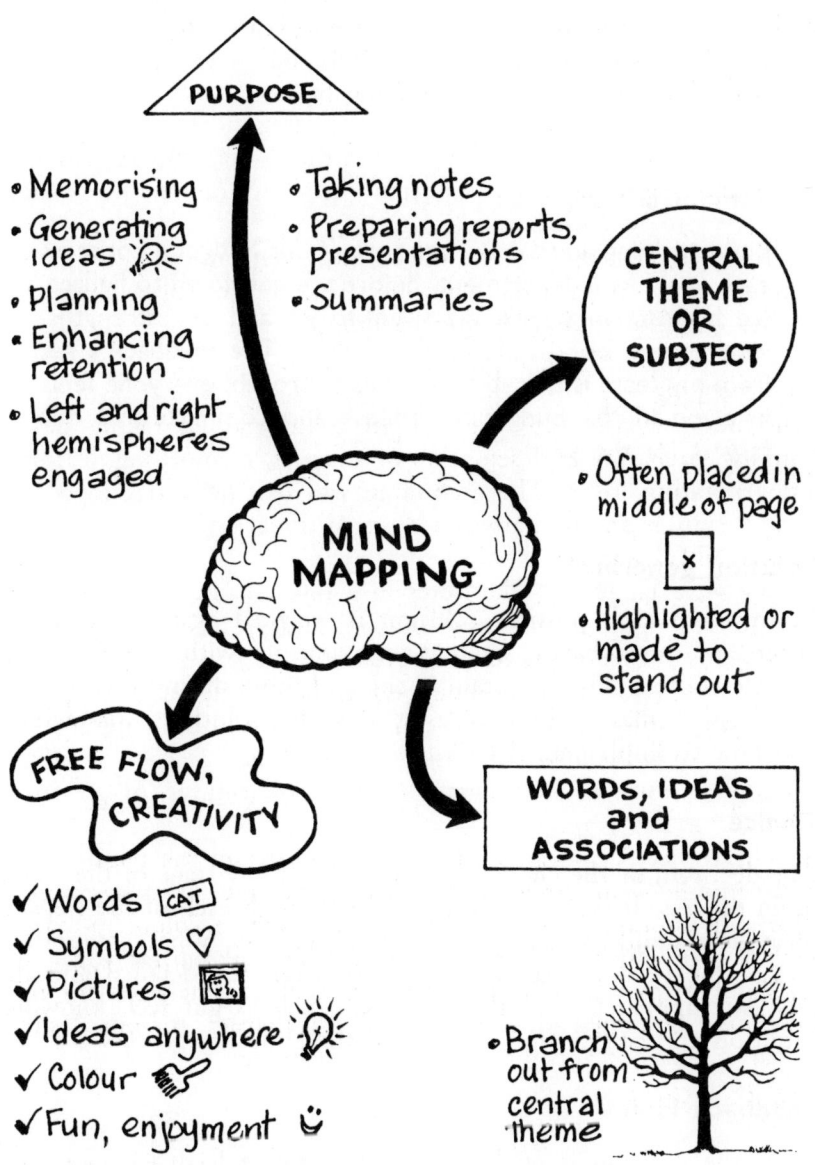

one assess them according to their strengths (S), weaknesses (W), opportunities (O) and threats (T) in relation to the decision.

SWOT works best in the same environment and using the same guidelines as ideas generation. In recent years, it has been used extensively in strategic planning sessions, but it can just as readily be used in any major decision making process.

Samantha's story . . .

Brainstorming and SWOT are part of our budgeting process each year. As a department, before we get down to figures, we brainstorm where we want to go and our strengths, weaknesses, opportunities and threats. The feedback I get from my team is that, by using this approach, everyone feels involved in the budgeting process and committed to our targets for the year.

Solution generator

In this step each possible solution is weighed against the list of criteria or 'must haves', so that we come up with a short list of feasible choices. The left brain is engaged more during this stage of the decision making process, as it looks for solutions, distinctions and how to implement decisions.

Choice

The decision, or the choice, can be made at any stage of the whole brain process. It is not necessary to go through each of the steps of ideas generation, SWOT and solution generation. What is important is that the final choice is balanced between the detailed and the wholistic approach, and that elements such as gut feel, knowing, intuition and compassion are part of the choosing process.

Feedback loop

Once the decision is made, we need to put a feedback loop into place. The critical elements are:

• Make an initial commitment to the choice.

- Take positive action steps to ensure that you attain your outcome.

- Make corrections along the way based on internal and external feedback.

- If necessary—for example, if your first choice is not meeting your outcomes—return to the decision making steps and make another choice.

A great example of this is learning to catch a ball.

Do you remember what it was like? If not, watch how small children learn this skill.

At first, it requires a lot of intense concentration on the positioning of your hands, watching the flight of the ball, being ready for the weight of the ball, and experiencing lots of dropped balls.

After a certain number of successful catches, the brain seems to click into place, and the process of catching becomes automatic.

It's here that the feedback loop becomes critical, so that you get finer distinctions about speed, height, direction, how far you have to move to catch the ball, and so on. For some people, this skill always remains awkward; for others, it becomes unconsciously natural.

A NEW DIRECTION

We have suggested that women have a natural preference for right brain activities. Jannie Tay[14] reinforces this when she claims that, in the area of decision making, women have an 'inbuilt natural edge over men'. And that edge, she claims, is that women are more intuitive and creative than men. Jannie goes on to say that women who are able to combine their natural use of the right side of their brains with the traditional decision making process, will think more wholistically and be better decision makers.

Celestine Michel, a business consultant specialising in strategic planning, talked to us about her approach with client organisations. In facilitating the development of strategic and business plans, she concentrates on integrating right and left brain decision-making processes. For her the key to the integration is consciously keeping people in right brain mode for as long as possible, because the left brain will come through naturally—we are so conditioned in the business environment to do it that way.

A lot of people will pick up the last balance sheet or company report to get a vision. If they're financially controlled then the vision is a greater return on investment or moving from an unprofitable situation to a profitable one. They don't have a vision of what kind of company they want to be, their place in the community, what sort of people they need to attract, and how many people. Many companies believe their vision is the ghastly, sterile statements that come out of their annual reports.

What we want to do is to delay the left brain in people until we believe that they have really opened up their understanding of what the business is or what the problem is or what the direction is. The left brain is not really a strategic, big picture thinker; it's a solution generator. We can't get them to think strategically unless we provide them with a process for doing this.

To open up people in this way, we use whatever right brain approach seems appropriate. We might use a brainstorm for a vision, a mind map to look at needs and wants, and SWOT as an ideas generator. With the SWOT process it's all about what other opportunities we have.

So what we do is encourage them to openly discuss their vision for the organisation and this immediately brings them into their gut feel about what they want. Once we've got them into this process, we can say to them, 'This is the heart of the business. Without the heart to an organisation's goals you won't pull it all together in the first place and you won't get the people going along with you'.

And what we get from this approach is total involvement. Everyone will participate, even the very left brain people. This is a wonderful way of teaching them how to come up with a much better solution in a far quicker time.[15]

We came across a different example of whole brain decision making when reading *Body and Soul*, Anita Roddick's book about the success of her company The Body Shop. From the beginning Anita and her husband Gordon have only done business in ways that maintain the strong values and integrity of The Body Shop. An example is their Trade Not Aid projects where they form business relationships with people in Third World countries. One of these projects required the sourcing of paper products that were acceptable from an environmental point of view. When a factory was sourced in Nepal, Anita flew in to look at the various samples made from water hyacinth and banana fibre.

I was delighted with the stuff and gave them an order for £25 000 worth of different paper products—mostly bags, notebooks, wallets for pot-pourri and scented drawer liners. It represented the factory's entire production for the next four months. Was it a sensible business decision for me to take? Absolutely not! It was loony tunes. But we are a company getting bigger and bigger and I was convinced that it was imperative to make such decisions in order to keep our soul. If we were not willing to get involved in these ventures we would have all our managers running around and getting incredibly excited about our profits, or the annual report, and forgetting that business is not just about performance but also about staying human. It was my belief that for as long as we, as an emerging multinational company, could concern ourselves with these micro-enterprises in the Third World, they would help to protect us from the perils of giantism and the inhumanity of big business. I felt it was these wacky little deals that kept us alive, kept the adrenalin running . . .

In this way we forged real links. They were happy because we were helping to expand the horizons of a traditional industry; we were happy because we were purchasing a product we knew we could sell. I loved the way these deals connected up—the way the sale of a product made from water hyacinth and banana fibre paper, on a high street in England, had a direct impact on the prosperity of a family business in Nepal, 6000 miles away. That purchase, and every purchase like it, assisted a community that few of our customers would ever meet and helped to protect an environment that few of them would ever see.[16]

Both of these business scenarios demonstrate, in very different contexts, the use of whole brain decision making. The necessity to learn to use and trust the valuable input of the right brain as a complement to and partner of the left brain is daily becoming more apparent in today's rapidly changing business world.

IN SUMMARY

How we make decisions is important for individuals, for organisations, and for our future. The values of the patriarchy have led us to believe that decision making is a logical, unemotional, left brain process. In practice, this seems not to be true for many men, and is certainly not true for the majority of women. Intuitively, women seem to make decisions in a different way from men. In particular, they are comfortable making more use of their right brains—using whole picture, intuitive, feelings-based processes.

The interesting thing is that, in order to succeed in the continuing rapid changes brought about by the information age, organisations need to trust and to use more right brain processes than they are accustomed to. The left brain cannot visualise the future, cannot give us a big picture view of a situation and cannot generate creative solutions.

With their natural preference for right brain, wholistic-thinking women can help to redress the imbalance, which has until now existed, between the way we have valued and the way we have used the two hemispheres of our brains. Correcting the balance will make an omnipotent contribution to decisions at all levels of organisations.

And these decision making skills can also be applied to how we choose to create our own futures . . .

7

CREATING YOUR FUTURE . . .[1]

'You can begin to create the future you want simply by recognising that you have the power to do it.'

The Club of Rome[2]

. . . BELIEVING YOU CAN DO IT

Do we as women believe that we can control our destinies? Do we believe we can create our futures? And who do we have to become in order to achieve the future we dream of?

Relatively, only a few women have so far achieved positions of high visibility and influence. Until recently, there seem to have been two main reasons for the 'success' stories:

Taking on the male mantle

Some of the key world figures of our time have been women who have assumed an inherited mantle of power from a male figure. Indira Gandhi, in the absence of a male heir, inherited the leadership of a political party and her country from her father, Jawaharlal Nehru. Queen Elizabeth II inherited the throne from her father, George VI, also in the absence of a direct male heir. Benazir Bhutto and Corazon Aquino succeeded male figures, Benazir from her father and Corazon from her assassinated husband. More recently, in Australia, Janet Holmes à Court assumed the leadership of a substantial business empire on the death of her husband, Robert.

Until they were thrust into this leadership role, the personal power of these women was invisible. But each of them has proved to be an outstanding leader in her own right. They have not only carved a future for themselves in history, they have also made a significant difference in the lives of the people they have influenced.

In the patriarchal system, this way of gaining power is acceptable. It is okay for women to gain power by default. But by their very success, these women have proved that it is possible for women to lead and influence. The way is open for women to choose this path of leadership and influence for themselves, in their own right.

And there are probably thousands more women who influence organisations, both large and small, via the men that control them. They do this without official title and without public recognition. These women are, and always will be, very powerful and should never be discounted or undervalued. They are creating their own future, although often in the name of a man.

Driven by passion for a cause

Other women who have been key figures in our own time, or in history, have been driven by an all-consuming passion or cause. Nothing else seems to have mattered to them except following their cause. Today Mother Theresa, Elisabeth Kubler-Ross and Alice Miller are outstanding examples; so too were Joan of Arc, Florence Nightingale and Amelia Earhart, just to name a few.

New path

We are now seeing a third path for women who are choosing high visibility roles in their own right. We have had some striking examples in recent times, such as Gro Harlem Bruntland, Prime Minister of Norway; Maggie Thatcher, Prime Minister of Great Britain; Golda Meir, Prime Minister of Israel; Mary Robinson, President of Ireland; and Anita Roddick, founder of the global corporation, The Body Shop. And we are gradually seeing more women in senior executive and chief executive roles in both public and private sector organisations.

> *'Aerodynamically speaking,*
> *the bumble bee shouldn't be able to fly*
> *but the bumble bee doesn't know it*
> *so it keeps on flying anyway.'*
> Mary Kay Ash[3]

The choice is yours. It is all about wanting to make a difference and believing you can do it. Belief in oneself is the foundation stone. From this point, you can consciously create whatever future you desire. This doesn't mean that everything will always go smoothly for you, but it does mean that your life and your work will take on a direction and a purpose.

So let's look at how you can create your own future. Once you believe you can do it, the next step is . . .

KNOWING WHAT YOU WANT

While believing that you can achieve is an essential first step, it is just that—the first step or the foundation stone. The next step is to gain clarity about what you want to achieve. While the 'whats' will not be fixed and immutable (but flexible), it is still important to have a clear idea of where you are heading. This knowledge will determine the path for you to take, the speed and intensity at which to move, a time frame, the feedback loop and how to measure success.

It is important that what we are going after is what we really want to achieve for ourselves and not because of the expectations of others. John Kehoe in his book, *Money, Success & You,* says, "There is no point in having goals that you think you probably should achieve, when deep down you don't really want them at all'.[4]

Most of the available information approaches setting goals and achieving outcomes in a very left brain, logical way. For example, research undertaken in 1953 at Yale University with a number of students showed that when asked if they had clear and specific plans on how to achieve their goals, only 3 per cent indicated that they had and that their goals were in written format. Twenty years later, when interviewed again, the same 3 per cent were found to be financially better off than the remaining 97 per cent who had not written down their goals.[5]

This evidence, although only measuring financial worth, has since been the basis of thought that all goals, if they are to be achieved, must be committed to paper. This has, to many, become the 'right' way. It also happens to be a fairly left brain way of achieving outcomes in life!

As we have talked with successful women, we have discovered that, while they have a clear and passionately held vision of where they want to go, they have not always written down their goals. It seems that the act of writing down goals might not be as critical as having clarity and passion about what you want to achieve.

So, whether you write your goals and plans down or not is an individual choice. If you choose to write them down, then try these strategies:

Format: express your outcomes positively and in the present tense and active voice. For example: 'I am making $150 000 a year', or 'I am the author of several successful books'.

Mind mapping: this is a really creative and enjoyable way of writing outcomes, especially if you use lots of colour. Not only is the right hemisphere stimulated by the colour and spontaneity, but also the left hemisphere becomes activated by the action of writing things down and planning.

If you choose not to commit your goals and plans to paper, then use all your senses when formulating them. Ask yourself questions such as:

'What will it feel like when . . . ?'

'What will I be seeing, hearing, touching when . . . ?'

Again, express your wants in the positive, present tense and active voice.

PLANNING YOUR FUTURE

Very few of us have the driving passion of a Florence Nightingale or a Joan of Arc. For most of us, our future direction seems hazy and unclear. And yet we all have the potential to become people of purpose and direction. It is only a matter of knowing how to do it. So here are some suggestions for eliciting your wants and desires.

Visioning

A vision is an expression of our purpose, what we feel passionately about, what drives us and what motivates us in a 'big picture' sense. It assumes that we have the power to shape the kind of future that we want. It is a clear description of what we desire in our life, in our career or in our business.

> *'Without a vision, the danger is that most of us will continue to perform at a set level, one we feel unconsciously is correct for us. If we exceed that level of performance, we usually will sabotage ourselves later on to maintain our "average". The importance of having a strong vision is this: If we visualise ourselves performing at a much higher level, our unconscious minds will interpret that as the new level of expected performance and will cause us to correct positively toward the vision without harmful repercussions.'*
> Dudley Lynch and Paul L. Kordis[6]

Visioning is a right brain process, and lends itself to freewheeling brainstorming and mind mapping. We see it as a kind of fantasy or day dream. If you are developing a vision for your career, then fantasise about your aspirations and your passions. If there are no holds barred, and you know you can achieve your wildest dreams, then what can you see yourself doing?

Carmel Niland had a very successful career as Women's Advisor to the New South Wales Government and President of the Anti-Discrimination Board, before setting up her own consultancy. She told us what was important for her in creating her own future:

I've always believed in the power of vision. Visualising what I am going to do and how I'm going to do it. I call it day dreaming—being away with the fairies—and I do it all the time—about 30 times a day. It doesn't matter what I'm doing—driving the car, talking to my mother-in-law, in a meeting where I'm just sitting there doodling away—I day dream. And I day dream in the Walter Mitty style—by moving into various characters and scenes.

And I write things down. If you know me at all, you know I love poetry and I use symbols and poetry a lot. I use them to get insight.

What's also important to me in visualising my future is remembering the messages given to me as a child and to cut across the limiting self talk—to be conscious of the negative messages and jettison them, and just hang on to the ones that are true for me—the expansive ones.[7]

To practise the skill of visioning, try the exercise on 'Visioning' at the end of this book (see p.201).

Goal setting

Once you have a clear vision of what you want to have, do and be, then the next step is to decide on a specific direction for getting you there. In order to do this you will need to evaluate your abilities, your potential, and the 'freeways' and 'roadblocks' to achieving your outcomes.

Refer to figure 7.1 as you read.

Abilities. Becoming more precise and objective about your abilities allows you to more clearly choose the path you need to take. Your abilities include:

• your strengths in the context of what you want to achieve. What age, health, skills, education, experience, resources (friends, contacts, money, etc.) do you have now (actual) and do you need (potential) in order to fulfil your desired outcomes?

• your perceived weaknesses. By looking at your weaknesses as well as your strengths, you are able to get a clearer picture of what might be holding you back from getting what you want.

One way to approach this step is to do a SWOT analysis on yourself (see chapter 6). Get input from friends, colleagues or family members whose opinions you value. Their assessment of your abilities and potential may astound you!

Figure 7.1   Goal setting

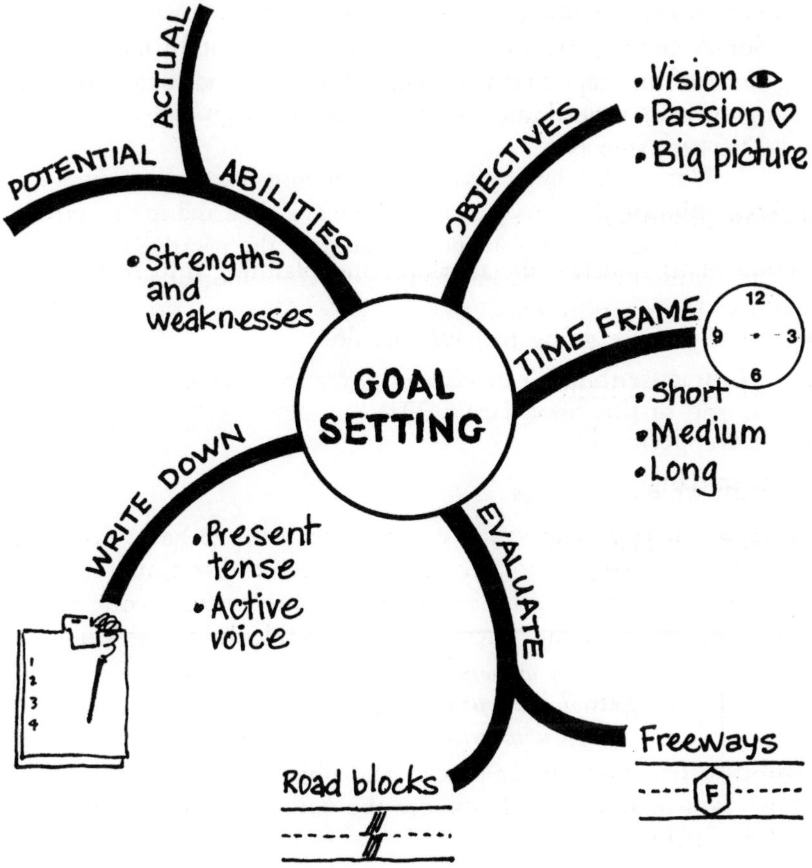

Source: Originally created for K. Chater and R. Gaster, *Trainers Guide to 'Breakthrough: Beyohnd the Glass Ceiling.'* (video)

Time frame. State your goals according to how far into the future you want to achieve them:

long term—ten years or more
medium term—up to three years
short term—up to twelve months

Feedback and evaluation. This is the process of checking along the way to ensure whether or not you are on track. So many people give up because things don't turn out the way they expect them to.

Yet achieving goals involves clear sailing (freeways) at times and rough weather (roadblocks) at other times.

Sometimes the process of feedback and evaluation means changing some of the steps that you planned to take, and it can also mean changing your time frames or even your goals.

The next step is . . .

Action planning

Action plans translate the thinking and planning into reality:

- what you are going to have, be, do

- when, specifically

- how, specifically

- with which resources

- who can help you

> 'Vision without action is merely a dream
> Action without vision just passes the time
> Vision with action can change the world.'
> Joel A. Barker[8]

Action plans (figure 7.2) create the stepping stones to achieve your vision. This is the stage where a bit more of the left brain, sequential, step-by-step processing comes in to complement the vision created by the right hemisphere.

Being specific about what you want enriches the process. For instance, on several occasions during the writing of this book we discussed what the cover of the book would look like (the colours, the lettering, the symbols). We imagined how we'd feel when it was published and a popular seller, and we joked about what we'd wear to the media interviews and what people would say to us.

Here's an example of the goal setting and action planning that we used in writing this book:

The vision. We have a shared and passionate vision for a world

Figure 7.2 Action planning

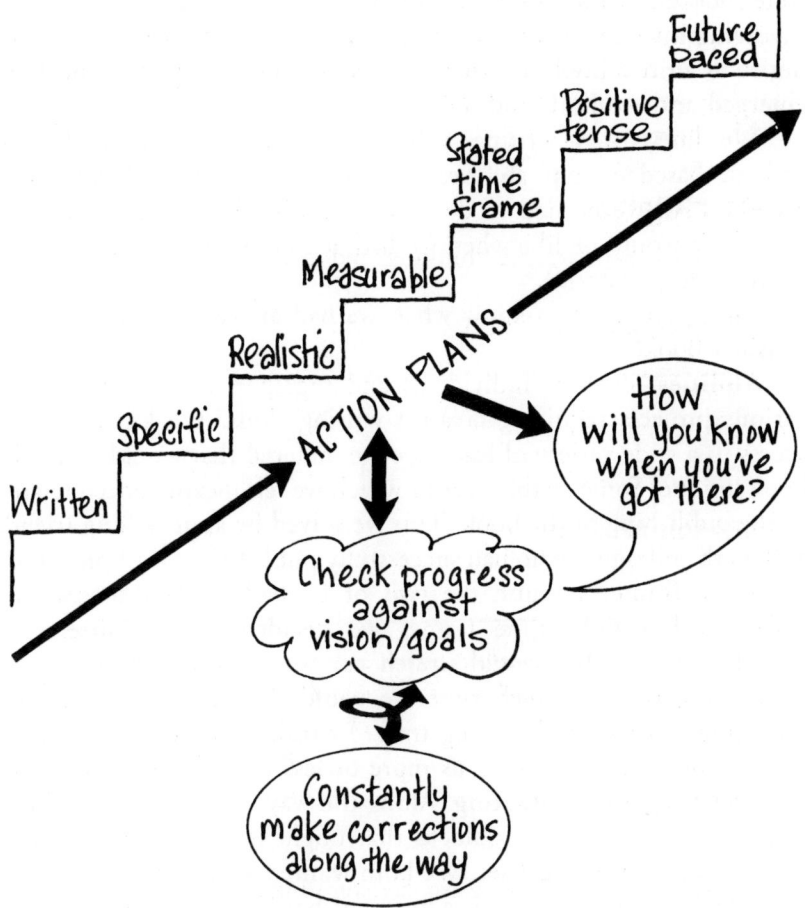

Source: Originally created for K. Chater and R. Gaster, *Trainers Guide to 'Breakthrough: Beyohnd the Glass Ceiling.'* (video)

where the contributions of women and men are valued equally. A world where, no matter what our age, sex, colour or religion, each of us has the possibility of fulfilling our potential because we choose to and because we are encouraged to by unrestricted, de-stereotyped, unbiased, forward-thinking people. As we have become clearer on what needs to be said—by reading, writing and talking to others— we have become more and more passionate about our vision.

The goal. Our outcome was to write a book together. Separately we had both wanted to write a book, but the topic and the timing were not clear for either of us. Working together on a project involving a video for career women gave us a focus and created the desire to write a book together. And suddenly the topic for the book emerged and we both had a *knowing* that it was 'right'!

We knew that writing a book together was achievable and realistic based on our abilities and the work we had already done together. All we needed to do was to continue to remind ourselves of what it would be like when we had achieved our outcome (future pacing; see p. 125–6).

And it was easy to know when we had arrived at our goal—the finished book!

Abilities. Both as individuals and together we had worked on various projects requiring creative writing skills. We knew we had access to a wide variety of leading edge material that would make the book unique. Some of the areas in which we felt inexperienced related to the publishing of the book. This we solved by approaching friends and work colleagues who had successfully published at least one book.

Time frame. Because the two of us had worked successfully before within tight time frames we decided to set ourselves a completion date that would stretch us. Within this time frame we knew roughly how much time we could devote to each chapter, including research and writing time. In reality, the time frames for each chapter varied, leaving us more or less time for other sections.

Checking and evaluating. Along the way we communicated any potential problems or roadblocks that might interfere with the time frames and plans we had set. We both wanted as smooth a process as possible and worked towards achieving that. It would be unrealistic to say we did not encounter some hiccups along the way. We did, and fortunately we resolved them and kept going.

We made constant corrections to the content of each chapter of the book. While the final chapter outlines bear only a minor resemblance to our original mind maps, those first passes at mind mapping were important as they helped us to get the writing process going.

Written goals. We didn't approach the planning process in the conventional left brain way. Instead, our first written approach was in the form of Post-it™ notes. And throughout the writing of the book we had heaps of fun brainstorming, mind mapping, and having lots of zany right brain sessions. Every time we had a block we chose to go into a right brain creative activity—and, without fail, it always worked. We learnt to trust that the ideas and the words would come.

Importance of flexibility

As you move towards your goal it is vital that you give yourself flexibility and room to manoeuvre. Many a goal or vision has been lost because of rigid and inflexible plans. Carmel Niland puts it this way:

'Set your goals in cement and your plans in sand.'[9]

Plans are not an end in themselves, but are a way of achieving dreams. They need to be adjusted and corrected until they give you the outcome you want. By developing a flexible approach you open up your life to more possibilities. Trial and error will lead you to what works best for you!

> *'Whatever humans have learned had to be learned as a consequence only of trial and error experience.*
> *Humans have learned only through mistakes.'*
> R. Buckminster Fuller[10]

Imagine the amount of detailed planning, both in human time and computer time, that goes into a successful space mission. Yet, on its voyage to outer space a spacecraft is rarely travelling a straight line from launch site to target. As figure 7.3 illustrates, the journey is typically one of correction after correction which, when plotted, looks like a zigzag path (see p. 120).

As humans we act in a very similar pattern to the spacecraft when moving towards our goals. Rarely are we 100 per cent on course. Sure, there are times when we get what we want immediately and without need for correction. Most of the time, though, we need some sort of feedback mechanism to keep us on track.

Just as the whole brain decision making process recommends a

Figure 7.3

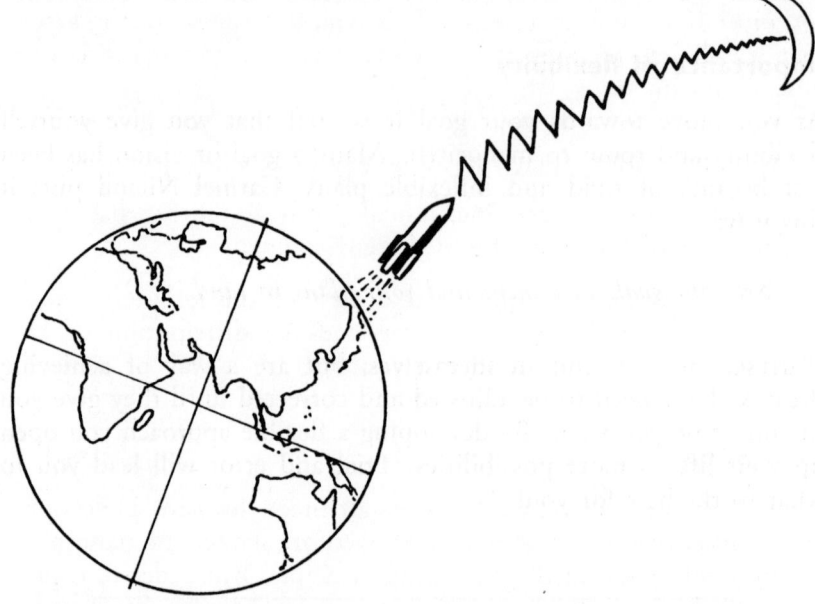

Source: Excellerated Learning Institute

feedback loop, so too in goal planning feedback will tell us when we are on and off course. For this we need to:

- know where we were when we started
- know where we want to go (our outcome)
- correct when we get off track
- know when we have reached our target (achieved our outcome)

WHAT IS IMPORTANT—THE JOURNEY OR THE DESTINATION?

All too often we become obsessed with the end result and forget to enjoy the journey (the process). The structured left brain drive to achieve an outcome at all costs can even take away any incentive for setting out in the first place.

What is the point of reaching an end goal if along the way there is no room for enjoyment and learning? What do we end up with? If we use as an example a typical business in the system that we all live in, then it seems that what we end up with is an obsession with:

- winning at the expense of all competitors

- making an ever-increasing annual profit at the expense of the majority of humankind and the environment

- achieving economic growth regardless of the long-term consequences to the global economy and the distribution of vital resources, including food and wealth

Precession[11]

R. Buckminster Fuller, who was an architect, futurist, philosopher and mathematician as well as an inventor, looked to patterns in nature (which he called 'generalised principles') in order to explain human behaviour. Bucky, as he has become known, distinguished the 'process' of the journey from the 'end' destination (or outcome) very clearly. To demonstrate this he used a metaphor from nature to describe what happens when we as humans set out to achieve a goal.

The analogy he made was that of the honeybee whose daily goal (the destination) is to collect honey and return with it to the hive. Along the way (the process, the journey) the honeybee is also doing nature's job of collecting pollen on the sacks of its legs and cross-pollinating from one flower to another. In this way, at an angle different from what the bee considers to be its goal, another more life-sustaining process is going on. The bee's true purpose, as Bucky put it, is cross-pollination. He called these side-effects or ripple effects the generalised principle of precession (see figure 7.4).

A major key is that you need to be in motion—going towards something or someone—in order to be able to influence the kind of ripple effects that happen around you. If you are stationary, then precession can still be going on around you because of the actions (motion) of others. The difference here is that you are caught up in the effect of *their* ripples, someone else is in control, much like

Figure 7.4

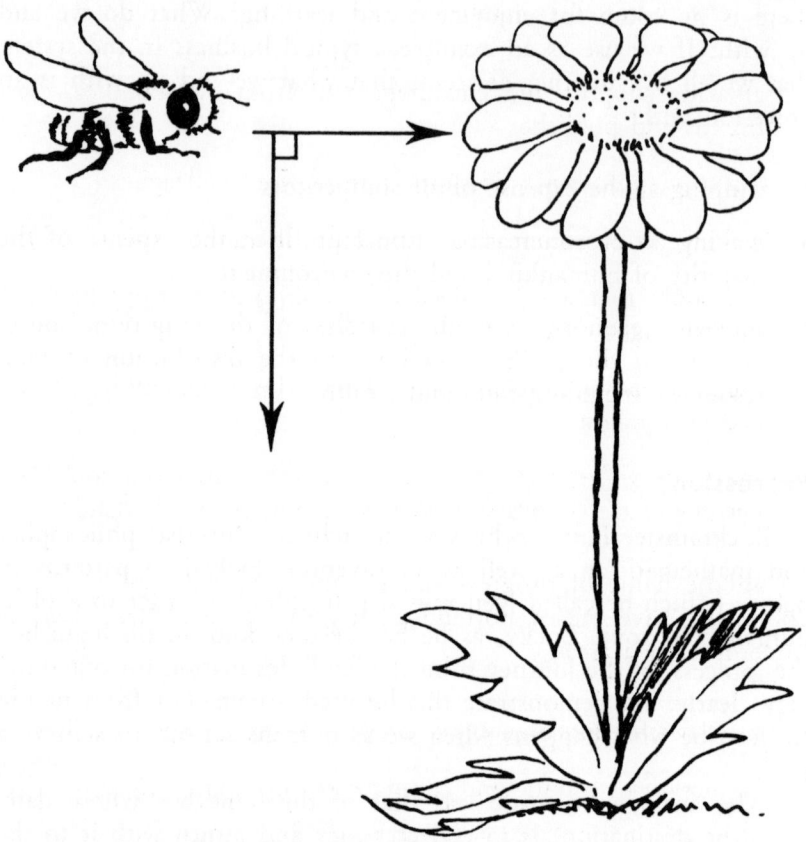

Source: Excellerated Learning Institute

the victim who says 'poor me' all the time, but does nothing to change what's going on. By simply getting moving you become able to at least play some causal role in what sort of precession occurs in your life.

Buckminster Fuller called humans 'honey-money-seeking bees'. Every time we decide on a goal, we set in motion a process of ripple effects. The trouble with us today is that we have become so obsessed with the destination—achieving the end—that we can't or don't even know how to enjoy the journey. What's more, we rarely get to notice what happens along the way—the precessional effects.

Ever since we started writing this book, a number of positive ripple effects started to happen for us:

- amazing support and encouragement from our families, close friends and publisher

- unexpected enthusiastic support from work colleagues

- we have both become more computer literate

- the books that we have needed have jumped into our hands at just the right time

- the women we have interviewed have been incredibly positive and encouraging

- the more we've worked on the book, the easier our jobs have become as our resource bank has become so much richer

In the name of progress and economic growth, some mining companies have caused horrendous negative precessional effects in underdeveloped areas:

- mass destruction of natural forests

- extinction of unique and irreplaceable flora and fauna

- irrevocable damage to local traditions and cultures

- pollution of waterways

- importation of new diseases that are often lethal to the local inhabitants

So how do we apply precession to individual outcomes?

Going towards a goal without noticing ripple effects is like stumbling blindly along a dark path. Noticing the ripple effects going on around you helps to illuminate the route and keep you on track—it enriches the journey. When you're on track, you will find that there will be lots of positive ripples. When you're off track, some negative side-effects will be occurring. Use this knowledge on precession as a feedback mechanism.

ACKNOWLEDGING YOUR WINS

While achieving a goal is highly motivating, the journey itself is often unrewarding for people. So why not consciously pause and acknowledge the wins that you have along the way?

Wins are the positive ripples that happen in everyday life. They can be helping someone in need, writing a letter that touches the essence of a communication, putting together a really good proposal, clinching a major contract. Wins are also getting the kids off to school and getting to work on time every day—the little things as well as the big things. It's the little wins that are so easy to overlook. And this is especially true for women who cope, often without thinking about it, with multiple jobs. We tend not to recognise what we do well. We manage households and families and jobs and rarely stop to acknowledge ourselves for this, and to build on these successful patterns.

So how do you acknowledge your wins?

Tell yourself what a good job you've done, pat yourself on the back, give yourself a treat or reward (and include someone else!), have fun—celebrate! Get external validation as well—it really feels good when someone else (sincerely) tells you what a good job you've done or what a great person you are. By doing this, you are making an ally of the unconscious part of you that rarely receives acknowledgment.

Try it! The more you acknowledge your wins, the easier it is to do and the more wins there will be to acknowledge. Once you can recognise and acknowledge your personal wins, it is easier to anchor yourself to success.

ANCHORING TO SUCCESS

Behavioural research has given us many distinctions about refining our behaviour and optimising our performance. One of the most useful of these distinctions is anchoring.

Anchoring is when a stimulus or a trigger causes a certain, consistent response. There's nothing new about anchoring. We all do it unconsciously, and it works for us both positively and negatively:

- when we see a police car and automatically check the speedo and slow down a little

- when we hear a particular song from our past and it makes us feel happy (or sad)

We have all seen examples of anchoring in sport:

- tennis players bouncing the ball before they serve, or rocking from side to side before they receive

- golfers swinging their hips and settling into position before hitting the ball

- swimmers, before they are called to the starting block, shaking their arms, hands and legs

In his well-known stimulus-response research on dogs, Pavlov was using anchoring when he made the dogs salivate at the sound of a bell.

Any stimulus can be used as an anchor—sight, sound, touch, smell, taste, past memories and experiences. The question is—how can we use this knowledge so that we can consciously choose to anchor ourselves to a useful resource state? And how can we anchor ourselves to success?

To learn how to develop the skill of anchoring, try the exercise at the end of this book (p. 201). You can use this powerful strategy in any future situations that are potentially difficult or where you want to ensure a successful outcome. After a while, you will find that you can go straight into your most successful state by triggering the anchor(s) that you have chosen.

FUTURE PACING

In business, future planning is used all the time for forecasting and budgeting. Fictitious figures are projected as if they are really going to materialise at the end of a certain time frame. On the basis of these figures, business plans and budgets are then worked out (and sometimes laid in stone). And people do not even register that this is a game of make-believe because they have been using it for so long!

In future planning, you look at where you are now and project into the future. Future pacing takes a slightly different perspective. You imagine yourself at some time in the future as if it is happening in the here and now and as if you have achieved whatever it is that you want to achieve. So the future becomes the 'now' and the achievement is something you have already done (the past). In *Influencing with Integrity*, Genie Laborde says: 'This small shift in perspective can produce amazing information. You act as if you are in the future. See, hear and feel your success. Then look back to find out how you achieved your desired state . . . Thinking backward is easier and more creative than thinking forward.'[12]

IN SUMMARY

Can you create your own future?

The answer is a most definite 'yes'! In fact, not creating your own future is actually a decision to allow someone else to create it for you.

IF YOU DON'T CREATE YOUR OWN FUTURE

SOMEONE ELSE WILL

You can plan your future by following the steps we have outlined in this chapter.[13]

- As we keep reiterating in this book, **belief** is the key. It is the foundation on which success is built. It is only when you believe that you can reach a senior position in business, or whatever else you desire, that you can start to plan your success.

- Once you believe that you can achieve, you can fantasise or day dream about what you want to achieve. Engage your right brain, and indulge in this process as often as you want. It will help you to develop your **vision** or sense of purpose.

- When you have a sense of what you want to achieve, the **goal setting** process—evaluating your abilities and potential, setting objectives and time frames for achieving them, and setting up feedback and evaluation mechanisms—will give you a direction, a way, to get there.

- **Action plans** are the stepping stones that translate the planning into reality. They deal with the specifics of how you are going to reach each of your objectives and should be specific, achievable, measurable, stated positively, and time-constrained.

- Remember to **acknowledge your wins** along the way. And celebrate all your wins—no matter how small!

- Choose to go into your most successful state frequently—by **anchoring** yourself to success.

- **Future pace** your results. From the perspective of future success you will be able to look back to the present and with the benefit of 'hindsight' see how to achieve your objectives.

Revisit your plans constantly. Part of the joy of life is the unexpected twists and turns that it takes. These twists and turns can open up opportunities of which you never dreamed. So be flexible and willing to continuously look for and assess options and possibilities, incorporate new fantasies into your vision and new directions into your goals and action plans. Become aware of the precessional effects of your actions, and use these signals as feedback.

The world around us is changing rapidly at the present time, and as it changes it is becoming clearer and clearer that the female voice is needed in business and world affairs. Women need to achieve a critical mass in high visibility positions as quickly as possible. We cannot afford the luxury of letting this happen naturally. We must accelerate the process. The most effective way that we know for doing this is to consciously create our own future—to know what it is that we want, to believe that we can do it and to go for it.

There are many people who have pioneered change and forged the way. Whether they are female or male we can learn something from them. They provide examples for us to role model. We don't have to reinvent the wheel. The examples they have set and the legacies they have left provide keys for us to accelerate the inevitable . . .

8

FAST TRACKING TO SUCCESS . . .

'Women who wish there were more female role models in business can perhaps draw strength from women leaders whose domain spans the complex affairs of an entire country rather than a single corporation.'

John Naisbitt and Patricia Aburdene[1]

. . . MODELLING THE SUCCESSFUL

A fast track way to achieving what we want in life is to model ourselves on others who are successful. Anthony Robbins says that

> . . . even when you have little or no background information and even when circumstances seem impossible, if you have an excellent (role) model of how to produce a result, you can discover specifically what the model does and duplicate it—and thus produce similar results in a much shorter period of time than you may have thought possible.[2]

As we said in chapter 2, there are plenty of male role models available for men, from their fathers and male relations to men in all walks of life—business, politics, sport, the arts, and so on. For most women this is not the case. The obvious female role models (mothers, female relations, teachers) have in general not given us a good sense of what can be achieved in the business world. So for women the strategies have to be different.

Men as role models

One choice is to model behaviour on male managers and leaders. This is a path that does work for some women, although they may earn themselves stereotyped labels like 'Iron Lady' and 'Queen Bee' along the way. But for many women such a choice does not fit comfortably with their innate feminine principles and modes of operating. The problem is, of course, that if we model the whole work behaviour of males, we may as well become 'female men'.

Yet, given the availability and diversity of male role models it makes sense for women to choose some as models. And one way to do this is to select and model the specific behaviours that are useful for us.

Carolyn Brand has spent her working life with only male role models at senior levels. While Commander of HMAS *Waterhen*, the mine warfare headquarters base for the Australian Navy, she explained to us how she learnt to selectively use these male role models in order to develop her management style and leadership skills.

Because I was lacking female role models, initially I adopted the male role models I had seen. I tried to mould myself on those models until I realised that I was trying to be something that I wasn't.

For example, one executive officer I worked under marched around the place giving orders and being cranky all the time. This is what I thought all executives did and I consciously modelled that behaviour in my first executive posting until one day I realised that it just wasn't working for me.

I sloughed off that particular role model and did quite a lot of research and read as much as I could about management styles and at the same time I studied other people that I knew to be successful that I had worked for. One of the particularly good captains that I worked for allowed me a great deal of latitude in how I did things. He would agree what had to be done but the means by which I got it done he left up to me. When I got it wrong and fell over he would pick me up and dust me off and point me

> in the right direction. This type of leadership worked in bringing me out as a naval officer.
>
> So I have used male role models in developing my style. But what I learned was to choose them carefully and blend them with bits which I sourced from within myself to create a style that works for me.[3]

Women as role models

Jannie Tay adopted a different approach to role modelling. When she started in business in Singapore in the 1970s, there were few women in senior positions, so she and her contemporaries used each other as role models:

> At first it was very hard for myself and other female colleagues to gain acceptance in the male-dominated business world. We had to be role models to each other and some of us were very outspoken, but we always retained our feminine qualities. The way we gained acceptance was by proving that we could produce a respectable bottom line, because that's all they ever concentrated on.[4]

A unique approach is taken by Meredith Hellicar, one of Australia's most influential business women. She believes that the very absence of women in higher positions is an advantage to aspiring women executives:

> By their very dint of numbers, men are often fearful of breaking away from the mould, while for women there isn't a mould and you often find that you take on roles that men would dearly love to have. You don't think about the fact that you're pioneering what you're saying or doing because there isn't any criteria against which to judge it.[5]

UNCONSCIOUS ROLE MODELLING

Whether we realise it or not, we have been modelling our behaviour on that of others all our lives. For all of us, parents and close relations are role models, as are teachers, family friends and perhaps also rock stars, film stars, book and cartoon characters, religious and sporting figures, managers and friends.

For most of us this has tended to be an unconscious process, and because it is unconscious it is possible that we have not been choosing the models who are best going to help us to succeed.

What is even more likely is that some of our role models have been imposed on us, rather than chosen by us. In our early childhood, we have little choice. We cannot choose our earliest models—parents or other relations, our parents' friends, or our teachers. From around the age of eight we start to look outside our immediate surroundings and choose people we admire as our role models. Then, we often choose an inaccessible person like a movie star, or a rock star, or a sporting star, and slavishly try to copy them.

> ### ALL SUCCESS CAN BE MODELLED
> ### AND CAN BE CHOSEN

CONSCIOUS ROLE MODELLING[6]

If our goal is to succeed in a career, or in life for that matter, it is important that we consciously choose our present and future role models carefully.

As we saw from Carolyn Brand's story, it is possible for women to select desirable behaviours and characteristics from male mentors. In doing this, they are not copying the whole male persona but are observing specific behaviours that work well, modelling these behaviours and then integrating them into their own innate style.

In the same way, when appropriate female role models are available, we need to be selective about the behaviours we choose to adopt.

Observing and modelling behaviours

In chapter 5 we looked at sensory systems (pictures, sounds, feelings) and behavioural flexibility as ways of achieving our desired outcomes through verbal and non-verbal communication. These techniques can also be applied to role modelling, so that we can be more precise about what behaviours we model and how we model them.

What do we need to look for when we model someone's behaviour?

- *physiology*—how they sit, stand, move, hold their head and arms, gestures (such as how they use their hands, eyes, lips, shoulders)

- *verbal communication*—the words they use (pictures, sounds, feelings), the tonality, pitch and volume of their voice, and the way they construct their sentences

- *behaviours*—what actions they take, specifically how they do things

- *dress*—what clothes they wear, their colours and style, accessories, hair, general impression

- *states and emotional responses*—what states and responses they have that are powerful and effective

- *beliefs and attitudes*—that empower them to take the actions which produce the results that you would like in your own life

The problem with so-called motivational sessions and groups who get together in order to urge each other to become more successful is that they only work at changing surface behaviours, physiology, emotional states or strategies (ways of doing and saying certain things). Even if they go further, by trying to impose new beliefs or values into the minds of receptive participants, the results tend to be short-lived because the person's underlying beliefs and attitudes are still running them unconsciously.

It is not until a person is capable of changing their old beliefs and attitudes into new ones that change can occur. Sure, people can be bullied, intimidated and coerced into doing new things and behaving in certain ways for a short time, but the driving forces that lie within eventually rise to the surface and take over.

This is precisely why the process of modelling includes the ability to determine what the personal beliefs and attitudes are of the person whose results you are wanting to recreate for yourself.

Modelling—chunk by chunk

The key to modelling the desirable characteristics and behaviours of a person who produces the results that you would like to get for yourself is to break down into small chunk sizes what it is that they do precisely. Then, link these specific actions to the beliefs that empower them to take the action that produces those results.

- Choose a model who is getting the results that you want in your life.

- Select the desirable characteristics and behaviours that produce those results.

- Notice precisely what occurs in small chunks, then link each action to a belief that allows the action to take place. Remember, no matter what we do or don't do in life, there will always be a belief attached to our ability to do it or not do it!

- Duplicate each chunk one at a time. Do not move on to the next chunk until you have the ability to precisely reproduce that specific action. Notice the belief that is associated with allowing you to take the action.

It is not necessary to have physical access to your role model, although if you can that's great! In the past we have both been able to role model people who we have had access to via videos and books.

From this type of conscious role modelling has come some of the most profound and long-lasting changes in people's lives. Both of us have experienced it personally and we have seen many women and men experience powerful changes by using the chunk by chunk process of role modelling.

As powerful and effective as it is, for many of us role modelling alone is not enough. We all need people (a minimum of one—and preferably more!) who can offer a guiding hand, keep us on track, open up the right doors and encourage us when the going gets tough.

MENTORING

Warren Bennis says,

> I know of no leader in any era who hasn't had at least one mentor: a teacher who found things in him he didn't know were there, a parent, a senior associate who showed him the way to be, or in some cases, not to be, or demanded more from him than he knew he had to give.[7]

And the same is true for women as we gain a critical mass at middle management levels and increasingly move into executive positions.

Michelle's story . . .

While I have always been stubborn and independent, self-confidence was a characteristic that developed slowly. Looking back, I realise that it was nurtured. I have always been supported and encouraged every inch of the way.

My parents were always 100 per cent behind me, believing that I could do whatever I wanted to do. They made it possible for me to learn the cello, sailing, horse riding, and to get my pilot's licence.

And certain teachers stand out for the way they encouraged my interest in learning, in music, and in sport. One teacher regularly took a friend and me to classical concerts, while another encouraged me to enter state-wide essay competitions. Yet another, a music teacher, allowed a couple of us to use her room over weekends—and this way we got our first introduction to classical music.

My first boss displayed remarkable confidence in my potential. In my first year out of university she gave me the responsibility of a major training assignment involving all head office staff, when I had never taught or trained before!

And today I am surrounded by family, friends and work colleagues who believe in me and I realise just how much this contributes to what I achieve.

The cumulative effect of all this support is awesome!

Not only is it a really effective strategy to have role models, but it makes sense also to consciously develop mentors and networks. Two American women, Verna Salmon and Amy Burgess, believe this so strongly that they have established Women of the World Mentoring (WOW'M) to offer workshops and a Community Action Program to help women to connect, learn from each other and share power through mentoring.[8]

There are many roles that a mentor can play. They can:

- encourage you and trust you with projects
- show the way and lead by example
- ease the path, introduce you to people and open doors for you
- teach you the skills you need
- tell you what you need to do and give you feedback on your progress
- share power with you by empowering you to succeed

> *'We need a brain to help us clarify,*
> *a shoulder to comfort us,*
> *and a kick to confront us.'*
> Natasha Josefowitz[9]

Many people believe that a mentor will pull strings for them. Our experience is that this is rarely true, especially for women. For example, Shirley Prutch, the first female to be named a Vice-President of Martin Marietta, a $5.8 billion American aerospace corporation, puts it like this:

> When I read anything on mentors they're always described as individuals who make sure that if there is a choice between two people for a certain job, that you're the one who gets chosen. Well, if that's what it takes for a woman to succeed, I think our whole system has gone to pot. Your success has got to be based on whether you can do the job and what you have done to show that you can.
>
> My personal definition of mentors are the people, men or women, who gave me a one-shot piece of advice or a lot of good advice, who helped me think things through or made me reconsider my own ideas.[10]

A mentor can be a friend or a spouse. For Melissa Cadet, Vice-President of the US corporation River West Developments, her husband, who has acted as a sounding board to her ideas and lent a sympathetic ear to her frustrations, is the closest she has ever had to a mentor.[11]

A critical attribute to look for, especially in the early stages of your career, is a mentor who is prepared to coach you. Here the role of the mentor is very similar to that of a coach in sport. Let's take tennis as an example. When you first learn to play tennis, your coach shows you how to hold the racquet, demonstrates the strokes, shows you how to move your feet, gets you to copy and duplicate every stroke, all before you even get to hit a ball! And as you improve, the coach gives you feedback and finer distinctions about the game and the way you play it. No talented sportsperson makes it to the top of their field without a coach. In exactly the same way, we need mentors to help us make it to the top in our careers.

For men, mentors who are influential in the organisation and who will open doors for them are often readily available through the old boys' network. It is an accepted way of business and of fast-tracking the progress of young men identified as future executives. For women, however, because of the relative inaccessibility of the male networks and the scarcity of highly visible corporate and small business women, the chances of getting this type of mentor are more remote. This is where networking is becoming more of a conscious choice for women who wish to advance in their careers.

For some distinctions on choosing mentors and role models, see the exercise on page 203.

NETWORKING

> 'Networking is becoming to this decade
> what consciousness-raising was to the last.
> It's a primary way women discover
> that we are not crazy,
> the system is.'
> Gloria Steinem[12]

Networking is something that men do particularly well. We are all familiar with the power of the old boys' network. Women have not yet developed equivalent mechanisms for providing support and encouragement to other women in the context of business. Ironic, given that female values and brain structure lend themselves to support and cooperation. Anita Roddick makes the point well:

I find particularly that women in business do not support other women, and I can't get my bloody head around that. I can't get my head around why. What is it about women when they are in senior positions? Maybe it's the male mentality of a corporation. Why aren't women working towards changing from a technologically and scientifically led mentality to one that is more intuitive and more caring and nurturing? I don't know the answer to that.[13]

Figure 8.1   Networking

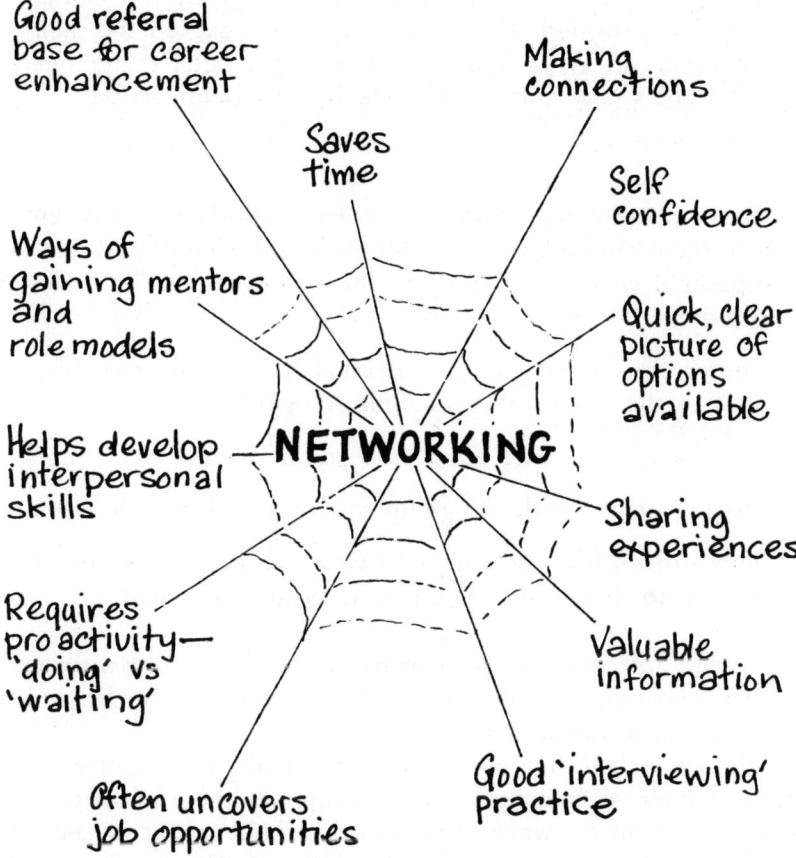

Source: Originally created for K. Chater & R. Gaster, *Trainers Guide to 'Breakthrough: Beyond the Glass Ceiling.'* (video)

Christine's story . . .

As Christine recently found out when she left her husband, support is one of the advantages of networking. Christine ran her own small business from home, and every day lost was critical. The day she moved house and office, a team of women (colleagues, friends and fellow members of a women's network) helped her move. They divided themselves into shifts, allocating time where they could around their own working days. By 8 pm the evening shift were sitting in Christine's new living room, enjoying the dinner they had provided. All the cartons were unpacked and their contents put away. Even the carpets had been vacuumed. Christine's new home and office was ready for action!

Even in networks which have been established by women for women there can be a tendency for exclusion, cliquishness and lack of support if you don't live up to their expectations. The rules are based on:

- conformity to the group; individual flair is only recognised as long as the group can gain some recognition

- reciprocity—you owe me if I do you a favour

- sharing success with the group so that the glory reflects on all

- only women who meet their 'criteria' can join and if you fail to live up to them after joining you become ostracised

Leonie Still gives examples of this in her book, *Becoming a Top Woman Manager*, and she claims that networking is not the panacea for all a managerial woman's ills.[14]

Having said all that, not all networks involve the negative aspects mentioned above. Many offer genuine support and act as an effective forum for aspiring women to advance their careers or personal business. As Laura Hwang, Vice-President of Women for Women in Singapore says, 'Networking is important—to keep in touch, share views and information, learn from others' experiences and find solutions, and, very importantly, for moral support'.[15]

A while ago we took part in an outdoor training exercise. One of the challenges involved crossing a swamp using barrels and planks. Our team found it a relatively easy exercise, involving mainly good balance and precision in the placement of the planks.

Halfway through the exercise, our facilitator said, 'Why don't you guys help each other?' We ignored him. We were managing perfectly well, placing and negotiating the planks one by one. A couple of minutes later he said again, 'Why don't you try helping each other?' So, for the sake of peace, we gave it a go, holding hands as we crossed the planks. And we found that, by helping each other, we crossed the swamp more quickly and easily. We could do it on our own, but we could do it better if we supported each other.

This is a good lesson for women. Perhaps we can make it on our own, but by giving and receiving support we ensure that others can make it as well. And, just as important, it *feels* good to achieve with others.

There are many formal and informal networks and groups of people around for just about anything that you can think of. There are women's associations to help and support women in management, professional groups, interest groups, and so on. And there are many benefits to be gained from belonging to networks that are appropriate to your needs:

- They provide opportunities to meet role models and mentors—both female and male.

- They are a way of meeting like-minded people with whom you can bounce around ideas, receive feedback and learn new and relevant information.

- Members are willing to be supportive and can help lift your confidence and self esteem during your rough patches.

- By drawing on the experience of others you may not need to reinvent the wheel.

- They are a forum to acknowledge your successes and celebrate your wins. For newcomers and people who work in isolation this can be extremely encouraging and supportive.

- Also for the loners and newcomers, networks can offer alternative sources for social activities.

- They can be the place to begin for those who want to become role models and mentors.

- Networks are also a great way of sourcing business or personal contacts—from job opportunities to financial advisors, from health practitioners to potential clients and training courses.

Networking has become important to successful career development. It is, quite simply, making contact with people who can help you grow—people with information and distinctions gained through their own personal experience.

Someone who, through networking and role modelling, built a very successful international leading edge training organisation with her two business partners is D. C. Cordova.

When we asked D. C. about her role models, she immediately referred to two of the networks of which she has been a part over the last 10 to 15 years. She also acknowledged her mother as someone who supported her with positive values and beliefs.

At first I didn't even look at role models—it wasn't in my consciousness. And then I actually modelled myself on men for a while. One man in particular was surrounded by women that he acknowledged as being very powerful and very beautiful. I used to look at him and say to myself, 'Oh, I want to be like them, but I want to be him'. These women never got to financially win out of the support and partnership they gave him to become very wealthy and well known. I wanted to be financially independent. That gives you tremendous personal power. If you have money in the world, you can do many things, especially to contribute to society. The other thing that happened was that, probably subconsciously, I decided that I would be a full-on partner with a man. And that's how it's always worked out for me.

And then it was really exciting because, yes, I did have a female role model a year later, Sondra Ray. I decided to change myself, to be the way that I wanted to be, and then I took certain aspects of her that I liked, like her clarity. She's powerful because she's so clear, she's done so much work on herself. So there aren't any surprises to herself about who she is. So I decided not to have any surprises either. It's very very seldom now that somebody can say something that's new to me about myself, because I know myself like the back of my hand. I think a lot of people are constantly surprising themselves and saying 'I didn't know that about myself', and that disempowers you.

Then there was one other female role model which was my mother. She was a single mother in South America in the 1950s, and she taught me to be totally self-sufficient. I never had the expectation that I would financially depend on a man, or any other person.[16]

WHEN YOU ARE SUCCESSFUL . . .

The current generation of women who have achieved high visibility see themselves as pioneers and as role models for the next generation. For example, Mary Robinson, speaking of her election as President of Ireland, said in a press interview:

I know that my election itself has given a boost, not just to Irish women but right down to five- and six-year-old girls, a confidence boost. I try in this office to be supportive and empowering of women.[17]

Influential women are also strong supporters of training and networking for upcoming business women. Jannie Tay is a co-founder and Singapore President of Women for Women, an Asian organisation founded in 1987 to encourage self-help among women in management. She sees herself as a role model for working women in the 1990s and makes herself available around the world to address conferences and seminars for women and to generally offer support and share her experiences.

As we take on more influential roles in organisations, we need to make sure that we continue to support those with less experience or ambition. Women with potential still frequently enter organisations as word processors, secretaries or clerks. They are often in these roles because of lack of opportunity, lack of education, lack of experience and their conditioning which, as we have seen, tends to reinforce stereotypical roles for women. Unless someone offers encouragement and strategies for self-development, their potential is often not realised. We both have seen efficient but underutilised and undervalued secretaries and clerks become, with a little support and help, highly successful business professionals—managers, salespeople, trainers, and so on.

Lee's story . . .

Lee was a 55-year-old clerical assistant working in the human resources division of a manufacturing organisation. She was given the opportunity to run the staff shop part-time—the shop was open to employees for two hours a day, from midday until 2 pm.

Within six months she had transformed the shop into a flourishing full-time business.

Twelve months later she had convinced senior management that the shop should be transferred to a street-front location and be opened to the public.

Be the person who sees and encourages potential, be supportive and helpful and, if necessary, be willing to fight to make opportunities available. No matter how tough things may have been for you, make the way easier for the next generation of women.

IN SUMMARY

Spend some time considering how you can accelerate your career and personal advancement by consciously choosing your present and future role models and mentors, as well as your support groups and networks.

There is a price to pay for high visibility and recognition in the world of business or for breaking old traditions and paradigms. For some the price is perceived as loneliness, for others the price is anxiety over taking the risk and the associated fear of failing.

Belonging to one or several networks and working with role models and mentors are all ways of minimising having to do it all alone. And not having to do it alone means reducing the risks because you have the benefit of other people's experiences and guidance. Patricia Forsythe, Member of the Legislative Council of the New South Wales Government, said of her career path, 'It was never a risk for me because I had a very strong role model. I had no doubt I could do it because she had already done it.'[18]

No matter how you choose your path, the road to your future will, from time to time, involve thinking on your feet and making decisions. With every decision there is a risk. Risk taking is unavoidable . . .

9

BEYOND THE COMFORT ZONE . . .

'The knowledge that you can handle anything that comes your way is the key to allowing yourself to take risks.'

Susan Jeffers[1]

. . . FROM CHAOS, DOUBT AND UNCERTAINTY

The decade of the 1990s began with confusion and economic chaos—for ordinary people in so many parts of the world, for business and politics, and for the environment. In the news there have been daily reports of organisations feeling the pain—the pain of losing profits, of capital investments gone sour, of bankruptcies, of the loss of valuable staff through redundancies or retrenchment. And it hasn't just been the small businesses that have been getting into trouble. Giants like IBM and General Motors have suffered. And some of the world's most talked about entrepreneurs of the late 1980s also fell victim to the burst bubble syndrome—Christopher Skase and Alan Bond to name just two.

To many of the people controlling surviving businesses, the times ahead are doubtful and uncertain. Change, very rapid change, has become part of life. Yet, rather than welcoming change (and acknowledging that confusion often accompanies the onset of change) what appears to be happening is a chronic reluctance to change with the times because 'it's too risky'. There appears to be a stubborn adherence to the old, a search for security by staying within a safe, known, comfortable zone.

Where this is most obvious is within the traditional organisation structures, which served so well in the past. These structures are now restricting our flexibility to adjust in today's rapidly changing world. We still witness male-dominated hierarchical structures. We still witness status reverence and obsession with the bottom line. We still witness suspicion of females in top executive positions. And we continue to witness a competitive, 'dog-eat-dog' world where typically the thinking and acting is local even though big business has become a global game.

Reluctance to take risks

No matter how many signs there are to pave the way for change, the 'status quo' reigns supreme in the minds of those who seem to fear the prospect of stepping into new territory.

Why is this? Is it because:

- they feel so threatened by the unknown, the possibility of a new paradigm?

- they have performance anxiety brought about by the thought of taking risks and failing?

- they are so comfortable with what's worked in the past, the existing paradigm, that a future paralysis sets in?

What is it about the human psyche that manifests in resistance to taking a chance and reaching into the unknown? And how come some people have such a problem in this area, while others freely welcome change and are prepared to take risks even (or especially) in the face of adversity?

On an individual level, we can go back to our values, beliefs and attitudes—the unconscious motivators behind our behaviours. We each have **acceptors** (tendencies towards risk taking) and **resistors** (tendencies that move us away from risk). The question we need to ask ourselves if we want to assess our risk taking tendencies is—do we have more acceptors than resistors?

Risk taking tendencies

	Acceptors	Resistors
Values	adventure, freedom, gainful achievement, flexibility, curiosity, trust, leading by example, new experiences	harmony, security, respect for status quo, hierarchy, power, loyalty, sameness
Beliefs and Attitudes	'I know I can make it.'	'This is too risky.'
	'I can handle it even if it doesn't work out.'	'Only fools take risks.'
	'Mistakes are opportunities to learn and grow.'	'I'm happy with things just the way they are.'

Very often, our ability or inability to take a risk will also depend on our **state of mind**. For instance, if we have a positive outlook, then whatever the result we will generally learn from the experience and put that new learning to good use in future adventures.

Anne Fairbairn is a poet, journalist and artist. With her husband, Geoffrey—who was a Professor in the Department of History at the Australian National University, specialising in revolts and insurgencies—she visited many trouble spots, including Vietnam, Northern Ireland, the Middle East, Pakistan and Zimbabwe. Her observations of intense suffering and violence led her, after her husband's death, to a decision to build bridges of understanding through poetry between cultures, especially Arab countries. This commitment has led her into risk taking and life-threatening situations.

After Geoffrey died, I kept asking myself, what's this suffering all about? What can be done so we can all understand one another better? So I decided to try to do something about it. My first trip took four months. I went to Egypt, Jordan, Syria and the Gulf to lecture in universities about Australian literature and to show slides of Australian paintings to give an insight into the imagery in our poetry.

I was invited to Lebanon in 1982 to talk in the university in Beirut and to collect poems for a book I was compiling. It was dangerous as it was during the Israeli invasion. I had to make a decision whether or not to put the trip off. Our ambassador in Syria warned me not to go. But because I'd set the plan and accepted the invitation from my friends at the university in Beirut I felt I must honour my commitment. The ambassador kindly sent me to the border in his car, and then I was on my own. I had to take a taxi and we drove down through the Lebanese Christian quarter. I asked the driver: 'What are those black things sticking up near the road?' He answered: 'Those are mines.' That seems, in retrospect, symbolic. For the thirteen years I've been travelling to Arab countries, there have often been bizarre things cropping up which often prove to be life-threatening.

For many years, even during the Iran/Iraq War, I travelled to Iraq. Once I arrived in Baghdad late at night after a long trip from Australia. Exhausted though I was, I woke up at about three in the morning. Against the light-haze of the city of Baghdad I could see what looked like a wounded aircraft returning from the front; it was trailed by a plume of smoke. Suddenly it shook violently, turned and plunged straight down. It was a multi war-headed missile and it exploded about 200 metres from my hotel. The whole building shook. In the morning I visited the site. A whole city block had been demolished by the missile. Soldiers were digging bits of people out; it reminded me of Vietnam during the war.

A lot of visitors left Baghdad that day. But I thought, 'If people are fighting a war and you accept an invitation to come it looks a bit discourteous if you go at the first hint of danger.' So I stayed.

Being your own person can be very lonely. You can feel isolated because you go against the stream. But I reassure myself that at least I'm not a 'cupboard' writer. I feel the tensions and the grotesque misery and this helps me understand the poetry of the day. My experiences in the Arab countries have enriched me. Going out to the frontiers of experience, both intellectually and physically, have made me discover a great deal about myself.[2]

Anne Fairbairn has a positive outlook. She has a purpose, and she accepts the risks calmly as part of the task she has set herself.

If, on the other hand, your expectations are pessimistic, then you are unlikely to succeed in risk taking ventures. For the pessimist this only proves that you cannot take a risk and win. And on the off chance that the risk does succeed, the outcome is often viewed with some kind of scepticism or cynicism.

> In the train recently we overheard a young woman talking to two men. She was telling them about her work.
> 'I'm a word processor, and I hate it. I find it just the most boring job.'
> One of the men asked, 'Why don't you get a different job?'
> 'I don't know what else I could do. And, anyhow, I always end up doing things I don't want to do.'

Pushing the norms, thriving on chaos and welcoming challenge is risky business. What is required is the ability to stretch beyond the known.

THE COMFORT ZONE

Doing something once does not mean that you will always do it that way. Doing it two, three and more times indicates that you are starting to become comfortable with your new behaviour pattern.

Have you ever noticed that the first few times you do something new you have to consciously choose to do it and think about how you are doing it? Then suddenly you start to do it automatically, without thinking. It is these unconscious behaviour patterns that form what is called your comfort zone.

Figure 9.1 illustrates the comfort zone. It is from this space that most of us live our normal, routine lives. Outside each and every comfort zone lie thousands of alternative options—the universal choice bank. Each time you take a risk and consciously choose to do something different you have the opportunity to expand your comfort zone.

We all have different comfort levels around risk. For example, Anne Fairbairn's concept of acceptable risk in her work in Middle East countries would be perceived as a high, and possibly unaccept-able, risk to many of us. For some people, hang-gliding or parachuting would be a real stretch. For yet others, leaving a secure job is uncomfortable to contemplate. For most of us, speaking in public is a huge stretch. Many women find the thought of pushing for a promotion or the prospect of leadership daunting.

The comfort zone explains why most people find change so shocking. They only feel comfortable when they stay within known and therefore safe boundaries. And there's absolutely nothing wrong with having boundaries. Quite the opposite—if we didn't have boundaries we'd be all over the place. It's when boundaries restrict us from being able to grow and experience new things that they are not always useful.

As long as you continue to act within your comfort zone you will choose the options that are easy and comfortable to you. By definition, you will not explore all the other universal options available to you beyond your own safety boundaries.

If you ignore the options and do not take advantage of new ways of doing things, then your comfort zone will not alter much over time. Your comfort zone will only grow beyond where it is now if you are willing and able to take advantage of the new options

Figure 9.1   The comfort zone

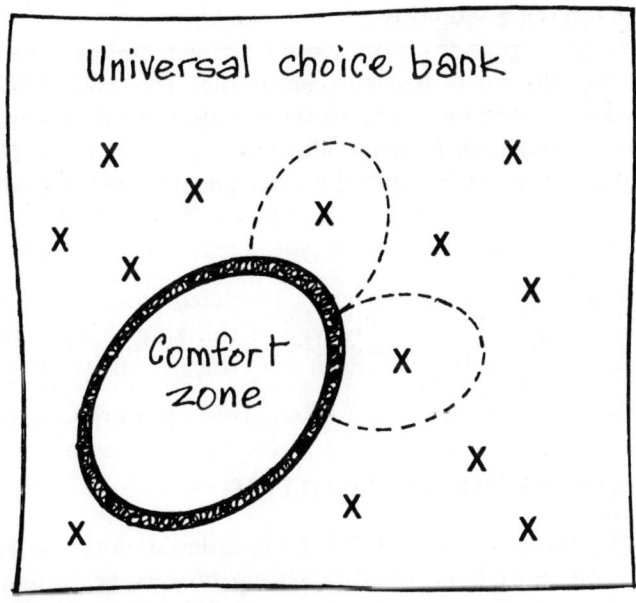

Source: Learning to Learn seminar, developed by Stephanie Burns

offered in the universal choice bank. (See page 205 for an exercise on expanding your comfort zone.)

Kerry's story . . .

I had left my marriage, moved to Sydney from the country with two small children and a dependent grandmother, and taken a job close to home as an economics teacher in an independent girls' school.

I discovered that the school ran on stress. This culture came from the headmistress, who believed in making life as difficult as possible for as many people as possible. It affected the students, and it permeated the staffroom like a bad smell.

After about 18 months, I decided to leave the school as I was taking the stress home and it was affecting the quality of our family life. Although I didn't have another job to go to and I was the bread winner of the family, I was confident that everything would work out okay.

My colleagues at school were horrified, and told me that they thought I was being irresponsible. They were locked into their mortgages and superannuation and, no matter how unpleasant daily work life was for them, they clearly found it a preferable option to the uncertainty of leaving.

The teachers in this story had a restricted comfort zone around career risk taking. And it is this type of thinking that has helped to produce a belief that is endemic in our educational system—a belief that if you make a mistake you have failed.

MISTAKES AS OPPORTUNITIES

Our entire education system has been founded on a series of rewards and punishments, right answers and wrong answers. Free, spontaneous thinking has not been openly encouraged in the typical Western education system until very recently.[3] What follows on from this rigid way of thinking is that it is definitely not okay to make mistakes. So you'd better not take a risk because it could turn out to be a mistake.

Small wonder that we see so few people, males as well as females, willing to 'go for it' and take risks.

If we want to set up a risk taking environment we need to create a belief system that allows us to see that:

> **MISTAKES = OPPORTUNITIES**
> **TO LEARN**
> **AND GROW**

ARE WOMEN RISK TAKERS?

You can almost bet on it that the people who go for it and risk beyond the norm, the pioneers and the entrepreneurs, are curious by nature. At school they may have been known as rebels or trouble makers.

Adventurous types of behaviour tend to be condoned and even encouraged in boys. We have already seen in chapter 4 that boys' games encourage risk taking. In general, the same sort of acceptance has not been bestowed on girls who have a natural curiosity and display adventuresome behaviour. They have tended to be pushed towards conforming, 'ladylike' and subservient patterns of behaviour.

Adventure and risk taking are traditionally viewed as the domain of the male. And yet, increasingly, we are seeing evidence that females also enjoy the challenge of risk. Given the opportunity, girls and women thrive on adventure-training activities such as abseiling, white water rafting and caving. Women were among the early aviators and astronauts, they have sailed solo around the world and now participate in all sports. They are pushing aside their conditioning and leaving unsatisfactory marriages, becoming self-supporting and, more often than not, also supporting their families.

Kathy's story . . .

With hindsight, one of the biggest risks I have taken in my life was walking out on my husband. It didn't feel like a risk at the time. I just knew that my marriage was so unbearable that I had to get out. I had a 3-month-old baby, and the only work I had ever done was as a doctor's secretary.

I was really lucky that my parents were supportive, and yet I still would have left that marriage even without their support. We stayed with my parents until my son was old enough to go to preschool.

My son has one more year of school to go, and two years ago I married again. But a very different sort of marriage. I am now my own person. I am financially independent with my own career and I own our flat.

As we saw in chapter 2, more and more women are moving into the area of small business. This is risk taking on a substantial scale. While the larger, traditional organisations offer less security to employees than they used to, they are still safer than setting up business for yourself. And not only are women going into the small business sector at a faster rate than men, they are also doing it more successfully.

While the stereotype is that women are not risk takers, the reality appears to be that we have a huge potential for successful risk taking! We have more hurdles than men to overcome—not only conditioning, but the whole weight of the patriarchal system contrives to push us away from leading edge, adventurous, risk taking paths. It is amazing that we have been as successful as we are!

> 'Risk taking is riskier for women—but you must do it
> if you wish to be recognised for your competencies.
> If you don't you will remain unnoticed.'
> Natasha Josefowitz[4]

To make the opportunities for success available to even more women, we need to develop some very specific strategies in relation to risk taking.

STRATEGIES FOR RISK TAKING

Doing something differently is a risk. Breaking new ground is a risk. Moving into a leadership role and setting up a new business is a risk. But these risks need to be taken by women if we are going to make a difference. The 'game' will only change if enough women are willing to stretch their comfort zones and plunge into uncharted waters.

So how, as females, do we go about learning to take risks?

The fast track way to learn how to take risks and minimise the chances of failure is to **role model** someone who is, to you, a successful risk taker. Notice everything about the way they go about risk taking. Also notice what they do when they don't succeed. Do they give up and throw in the towel or do they keep on going? When do they cut their losses and turn to something new? Notice specifically how they represent the world of risk taking to themselves.

For example, Anita Roddick does not see herself as a risk taker. She puts it like this: 'All you ever do in business is . . . the things that you know . . . It's no more complicated than that. I just do what I do well and keep on doing the same thing better.'[5]

Trust that whatever is meant to be will be for the best. Approach risk taking as a learning experience. Ask yourself, 'What is the worst that could possibly happen?' and trust that you can handle it. In her book, *Feel the Fear and Do It Anyway*, Susan Jeffers talks about becoming a lifetime student, where there is a lesson to be learnt from every experience, every decision and every risk you take.[6]

If you accept responsibility for your decisions and for their outcomes you are more able to control the process and to learn from each experience.

> '*Even though we are not 100 percent responsible*
> *for everything that happens to us,*
> *we might as well act like it and work with it*
> *because we are the ones*
> *who are going to have to live with the outcome . . .*
> *By taking responsibility,*
> *you gain the leverage that comes from staking a direct claim*
> *to the right to control the outcome.*'
> Dudley Lynch & Paul L. Kordis[7]

- In risk taking **timing** is everything.
First you need to do your homework and consider all the consequences. It might be useful here to consider some of the steps taken in the whole brain decision-making process (see chapter 6). Remember also that sometimes what seems a risk to others is not a risk to you because you just know or you have a gut feel that it will work out.

    Then, if you can get the timing right, you increase your chances of success exponentially.

Roma consciously chose to do a degree in Japanese and Economics in the mid-1970s. At that time, as it turned out, there were no real opportunities for women with this combination other than being an interpreter in some large corporation. It is only now, with the influx of trade and tourists from Japan, that fluency in Japanese is an asset. While the area was correct, her timing was too soon as far as career opportunities went.

Jannie Tay left the security of a family business in 1976 and set up her own shop, aimed at the luxury end of the watch market. This was a new and untried market. Her timing was perfect. That first shop was the beginning of The Hour Glass, a publicly-listed corporation which now has 15 outlets in Singapore, Kuala Lumpur, Jakarta and Australia, and which has also diversified into other activities.

- The more **experience** you have, the more you are able to contain the risk factor in any venture.
Take the stock market. For novices and amateurs it is highly risky, but for people who play it all the time, for a living, it is just that—a way of earning a living.

- Know what your **outcome** is—what you want from taking the risk, both in terms of the precession and in terms of the end result. Celebrate when you stretch beyond your comfort zone!

- Be **optimistic**. Expect the best, and learn to laugh when the second best, or even the worst, happens. Treat mistakes as opportunities for learning and growing.

Anne Fairbairn's intervention in the hostage crisis in Iraq shows these strategies in action.

I have made many friends in Iraq as a result of my visits over the years. So when the hostage crisis emerged, I felt that it was practical and sensible for me to try to help as nobody else in Australia had the experience that I'd had. That includes our diplomats, because they are not always able to get around very much, especially in a place like Iraq. But because I had become friendly with some quite influential people, not in the regime but in medical, artistic and academic fields, I thought I had a chance of helping the hostages. I took heart also from the success of a letter I had sent with Sir Robert Drew (an Australian who was greatly respected in Iraq because he had established the modern school of surgery in Baghdad in the 1950s). He took my letter to the Iraqi ambassador in London and it secured the release of all the women and children held hostage.

When I decided to fly to Baghdad, my sons said to me, 'Mum, you don't have to do this—it's risky,' and 'Whoever's going to thank you?' They were right on both counts. Because in the world we live in today people can never quite understand anyone doing things through an ideal or conviction rather than for remuneration. Not that that worries me at all. You don't do things in order to be thanked.

After I arrived in Baghdad I saw the hostages and made my plans. I have since been criticised for perhaps giving credibility to Saddam Hussein—a ridiculous accusation! I asked my Iraqi friends who I needed to see to ask if I could take the Australian hostages home. Willie Brandt, during our meetings in our hotel, was very supportive and gave me the courage to persist.

Finally I was taken to the speaker of the Assembly, Saadi Mehdi Salah. We spoke about pre-Islamic poetry for about half an hour, and then we got down to the nitty gritty. I said, 'I'm in no position to bargain or negotiate, but may I take the Australians and New Zealanders home?'

Regrettably, the day before I arrived, they put on the

'box' that video of the Australian sailors 'play acting' in Arab clothes on a frigate. He said, 'We have to be seen not to be weak about the insult to Islam.' And I said, 'Yes, I regret that. I think it's an insult to all Muslims and I'm in no position to apologise other than to say, as an Australian, I feel very ashamed.' Then I pondered on it a bit and said, 'May I ask you, would you consider my taking the older men who are sick?' And he answered, 'Yes, take the older ones.'[8]

IN SUMMARY

For most of us, risk taking is venturing into the unknown, moving out of our comfort zones and pushing against our conditioning. If you decide that this is the path you want to take, there are a number of steps you can take to ensure that your risk taking strategies are successful:

- Check your values, beliefs and attitudes and make sure that you have more acceptors than resistors.

- Increase your self-confidence by taking small steps at first. Once your esteem has grown you will find that your willingness and ability to take bigger risks increases.

- With an optimistic outlook, expect success and continuously move towards it.

- Regard mistakes as opportunities for learning and growing.

- Consciously make decisions that involve expanding your comfort zone on a regular basis.

- Build on each success by acknowledging your wins and anchoring yourself to success.

There are two kinds of organisational risk taking, both of which are important for women who wish to become more visible and to achieve success (however you define success for yourself):

Intrapreneurial

In the past, women have had a tendency to accept, to make things work, and to maintain harmony. This has been a factor in the longevity of the patriarchal system. It also makes women less visible because only those who are willing to go out on a limb are seen as leadership material.

It is time to acknowledge that women do have an innate ability to take risks, to encourage ourselves to think more positively about risk taking and to know that we will be able to assess when and when not to take them.

Entrepreneurial

The safety valve that women seem to have in taking risks has paid off for them in the area of small business. They tend to take risks more thoughtfully and carefully than men and these strategies are enabling them to have higher success rates.[9]

Just as they have different genderlects and use different decision-making processes, women and men also employ different risk taking strategies. In order to succeed in the business world, it is necessary for women to understand the male strategies, while not losing the strengths of their own approaches. For example, the female strategies are paying off well in the area of small business, and yet within larger, more traditional organisations women are not yet perceived as risk takers.

To most people, risk taking is a challenge. Leadership is also a challenge. The two seem to go hand in hand. If we are to have more women trail-blazers in the world, then we need to be prepared to step out of our comfort zones, develop a vision of where we want to go, become more visible and believe that our voice is vital to the future of business and the future of our world . . .

10

WALKING THE TALK . . .

'In the first decades of the third millennium we and our children will look back at the later half of the twentieth century and remark on how quaint were the days when women were excluded from the top echelons of business and political leadership, much as we today recall when women could not vote. How naive were the men and women of the 1980s, we will say, those people who believed in something called a "glass ceiling" and thought it would forever exclude women from the top.'

John Naisbitt and Patricia Aburdene[1]

. . THE CHALLENGE OF LEADERSHIP

You know leadership when you see it, when you hear it and when you experience it, but it is difficult to say exactly what it is. Some say that what it isn't is management—that managers focus on control, systems, structures and rules, on maintaining the status quo and on the short term. And yet it is true for most organisations that the managers (or some of them!) are also perceived as the leaders of the organisation.

For Warren Bennis, leaders are people who 'work out there on the frontiers where tomorrow is taking shape, and they serve here as guides—guides to things as they are and as they will be . . .'.[2] They have a vision, and can communicate this to others and gain their cooperation and support in reaching their goals. They innovate, develop, focus on people, inspire trust and have a long-range perspective.

In his book, *On Becoming a Leader*, Warren Bennis isolated six important ingredients of leadership:[3]

- Leaders have a clear **vision** of where they want to go, why they want to go there, and the persistence to get there.

- They feel **passion** for what they do and can communicate this to others.

- They exude **integrity**, made up of self-knowledge, deep-seated ethics, and maturity gained through experience.

- They are able to earn the **trust** of others.

- They have **curiosity** and are willing to ask questions and learn.

- They are willing to **take risks** and try new things.

And yet a person can have all of these qualities and still not be a leader, or only one or two of these qualities and be an outstanding leader. Position doesn't make you a leader. Being a prime minister or a president doesn't make you a leader, being the CEO of an organisation doesn't make you a leader, being a manager doesn't make you a leader. It's the intangibles that make the difference.

Meredith Hellicar, when she was Executive Director of the New South Wales Coal Association, told us what leadership means to her:

> To me the mark of a leader is somebody who actually does have a vision and then inspires that confidence, that trust, that even if they haven't definitively articulated the strategy for getting there, you feel as if they do know. Certainly the great mentor in my life inspired me with the joy of the journey and the feeling that he would find a way and gave me a sense of purpose and enjoyment to the whole journey. And that to me is real leadership.[4]

Where are leaders to be found?

Leadership is not restricted to the top levels of organisations or governments. Leaders are to be found at all levels of organisations and society. And, increasingly, in these times of chaotic change and uncertainty, organisations are finding that they need the personal leadership of individuals at every level of the corporate structure.[5]

Each of us has the potential for leadership. Whether we realise this potential or not depends on the situation and whether we are willing to accept the challenge. One of the problems is that, to date, too few women are taking up the leadership challenge. Women leaders are still the exception. The majority of countries have not yet had a female prime minister or president and the majority of employees have not experienced a female CEO.

While women continue to accept having less visibility than men, leadership will remain, in the eyes of most people, synonymous with 'male'.

WHY IS IT IMPORTANT FOR WOMEN TO ASPIRE TO LEADERSHIP?

The answer is really very simple. Women need to be in leadership positions to achieve visibility and power, as it is only with power and visibility that we can effect change. If you believe strongly enough that things have to change, then you must strive to get yourself into a position where you can influence change. In other words, you must get into a position of power.

> *'You can't change the organisation until you have significant power yourself.'*
> Professor Leonie Still[6]

For many women, power is a dirty word that smells of politics, underhand deals, corruption and perhaps even violence. Yet the simple dictionary meaning of power is 'the ability to do or act'.[7] How we use our power depends on us. We can choose to use it to control, to restrict access to information and to reinforce systems and conventional ways of operating, or we can choose to use it to empower other people, to change the rules of the game, or even to change the game itself. (See page 206 for an exercise on power.)

One thing is for sure. You have to be in the game to change it. Only the players can change the rules.

Notice the types of power being used by the leaders most visible to you. Are they modelling power in a way that enhances the 'ability to do or act'—power that allows elasticity and growth of others as well as themselves? Or are they using power in the forceful, manipulative sense where their needs are met above the needs of all others?

> 'We are in love with the influence of power.
> We need to be in love with
> the power of influence.'
> Michael Grinder[8]

Information has always been the key to power. Alvin Toffler claims that every power-holder 'wants to control the quantity, quality, and distribution of knowledge within his or her domain'.[9] The language and values expressed here suggest an older style patriarchal approach to control and power. Our experience is that women have a different approach. A more 'female' interpretation is given by Judith Vogt and Kenneth Murrell in their book, *Empowerment in Organisations*: 'Information as power, when it is shared, creates more power in a system that encourages and rewards collaboration'.[10]

Women—with their natural disposition for creativity, caring, interdependence, cooperation and sharing—are desperately needed in powerful positions and leadership roles everywhere, in all types of organisations, in politics, in society generally. The presence of women in key positions in sufficient numbers will change the way business is run. At the very least, we will bring more 'heart' into the day-to-day business world—more concern for others, more discussion and sharing of information, ideas and decision making.

WHAT ARE THE FACTS?

In the so-called 'developed' world, women now represent up to 50 per cent of the paid workforce and, according to United Nations' statistics, actually do two-thirds of the world's work. We are making headway at lower and middle management levels of organisations, but the key positions of power and influence are still eluding us. In the US, less than 1 per cent of women are in top executive positions, and this percentage is not increasing. In Australia, women represent only 3 per cent of all board members, and their representation on boards has not increased in the last three years. In England less than 1 per cent of the executive directors of publicly listed companies are women, and a survey by the *Economist* showed that only 4 of the top 100 establishment posts were held by women in 1992, an increase of only two since 1972.[11]

As we have already seen, the only type of organisation in which a different picture is emerging is small business (see chapter 2). Women entrepreneurs are entering small business at a faster rate than men in the Western world, and their success rate is better.

So why is it that more and more women are setting up their own organisations and are not moving into highly visible positions in traditional organisations? Are they choosing not to, or are they being excluded from these positions? Apart from small business, women are mainly to be found in leadership positions in voluntary, fund-raising and community-based activities. Is this because their real interests lie here? Or is it because these are the only areas where the patriarchal system has so far allowed them to hold leadership roles? Have women limited themselves by their values and beliefs?

Invisibility

A number of factors have contributed to the lack of women leaders. As John Naisbitt and Patricia Aburdene say, one of the problems is that not enough women are thinking like CEOs and like leaders.[12] Another factor is that female socialisation has tended to trivialise female ambitions and achievement needs, except when they are expressed through supporting a male. Male socialisation reinforces this by giving men an expectation that women occupy subordinate positions. And in these subordinate positions it is all too easy for women to be 'invisible'.

Carolyn Brand experienced the 'invisibility' of women early in her naval career:

> At Faslane, I was the manager of the tactics computer system and we were developing this interactive computer model for a new weapons system. I was the leader of the group and I supervised the contractors.
>
> It was symptomatic, particularly in the Royal Navy, that women were not considered able to do any serious-type

task. If there was a woman in uniform present then you knew automatically that she was probably a secretary or some sort of administrator, so that by her mere presence it was already indicated that she wasn't going to be a major player.

One of the senior admirals came to visit us and he seemed to me to be about 90 years old. He demonstrated exactly what I've seen in all the other admirals. As the group leader I welcomed him to the area, and then stood back and allowed my troops to put on the demonstration. Afterwards we lined up to answer questions and he ignored me entirely. He spoke to the petty officer; he even spoke to the able seaman, who was almost leaning on his broom handle, because one of his jobs was to sweep the floor. He tried all of them before he would actually speak to me because, as far as he was concerned, I was equated in the social sphere rather than in a work sphere.

Men like him had probably joined the Navy at 14, and their only experience of women was their mother, their nanny, their matron at school, perhaps their one or two girlfriends, perhaps women in a few ports and their wife and daughters. They had no experience of working with women and so they didn't know how to. Their attitude is based on their conditioning and their education. They just couldn't conceive of women in anything but subservient roles.[13]

It is understandable that many men find it difficult to accept the idea of women as CEOs and senior executives if they have never had to deal with women, other than as mothers, wives, daughters, aunts, girlfriends, nurses and secretaries. Men will only readily accept women as executives and leaders once a 'critical mass' of women reach leadership positions in organisations.

WHAT DO WOMEN BRING TO LEADERSHIP?

So what do women need to be and to become if we are to move into leadership roles?

The good news is that ideally what we need to be is ourselves.

No longer do we need to attempt to clone male leadership and management styles. As Alvin Toffler says, leaders of the future are likely to be 'more dependent . . . on intuitive sensitivity, empathy, along with guile, guts, and plenty of old-fashioned emotion'.[14] And their role will be less directive and more supportive, less content-based and more process-based, less rules and systems-dependent and more oriented towards flexibility, continuous change, innovation, self-management and lifelong learning.

> *'What business needs now is exactly*
> *what women are able to provide . . .'*
> Sally Helgesen[15]

In *The Female Advantage*, Sally Helgesen has published her research into the management and leadership strategies used by four successful American business women. The sample is limited. However, the pattern she reveals is consistent with our observations, with other recent research into female leadership styles and with the comments of many successful business women. And it demonstrates some interesting contrasts with the traditional male style.

Sally Helgesen found that:[16]

- Women focus on **relationships** and the **process of** work. Men focus on tasks, especially the completion of tasks and the achievement of goals, sometimes at the expense of people and relationships.

- Women are '**big picture**' and **long-term oriented** and the big picture includes not just work but all the facets of life, including the family and the environment. Men have a sharp focus on the everyday, on 'fire fighting' rather than on reflecting.

- Women see their jobs as just **one part of their identity**, with all the parts flowing together to create a whole. This allows them to look at their work roles in a detached way, to assess work priorities against other parts of their lives, to be more flexible in their approach to issues and to play whatever role is called for in a given situation—negotiator, counsellor, boss, mother, friend, and so on.[17] Men, on the other hand, tend to identify themselves with their positions. They gain prestige and status from their positions, and seem less able to detach themselves from their role as manager.

- Women tend to see themselves as the **centre of a network of information**, and are able to acquire and share information and decision making freely. In contrast, men see themselves at the top of a hierarchy, and tend not to delegate decision making. They regard information as the chief source of their power and are reluctant to share it.

Lara's story . . .

Over the years I have had both women and men as bosses.

My first boss, Margaret, became the standard by which I judge all other managers. She was the head of the sales division of a large textile manufacturing company. I was just out of university, and yet she treated me as an equal, shared information and discussed issues with me, and very quickly gave me some major accounts to manage. I really felt responsible for these accounts and never had the feeling of being watched or checked on, and yet she always knew exactly what was going on. She kept throwing challenges and opportunities at me, gave me room to move, and helped me to grow as a person. I was genuinely sorry when, five years later, I left to take up a management role in another organisation. Twenty years and quite a few organisations later, there are still strong links between Margaret and those of us who worked with her.

Recently, I had the misfortune to experience a totally different type of leadership. It was in a public sector environment and my boss, John, was the head of an autonomous, revenue-earning department. I was the team leader of the marketing division and John, as I found out later, was highly suspicious of the marketing function, feeling that marketing was a glamourous, unproductive role that made no real contribution to the bottom line.

When I was appointed, John was on long service leave.

The acting head of department who appointed me was just hanging out until his retirement, and he left me and my team alone. Six months later, when John returned, he instituted the petty rule of a tyrant and I found myself back in a 'boarding school' environment. For example, I had to get his permission every time I left the building to see a contact or a client and he insisted on making all decisions, right down to approval for the smallest petty cash vouchers. One of his specialties was dressing people down in front of other members of staff. Morale sank to a desperate low, and staff spent huge amounts of time discussing their dislike of John and of the organisation.

I tried to go above his head, but found that my complaints fell on deaf ears—there was no one to appeal to. Within six months, the team disintegrated. Some took extended leave on medical grounds while they looked for another job, and others just left. Amazingly enough, John is still there, in the same position, and the turnover rate in his department remains 'unaccountably' high.

A different voice

Women have seen and experienced the male model. And many women find that they cannot comfortably operate in the same way. In rejecting the parts of the male style that are incompatible with their own natural style, they are discovering that they have a different way of working and leading. The path to lower and even middle management levels often involves a compromise for women. However, as they move further up the organisational ladder, or set up their own organisations, they have the opportunity to develop their own voice, their own way of doing things.

An example is Anita Roddick, who declares her disdain for the traditional values and methods of business. She runs a highly successful global business based on the values of compassion, love and a sense of fun. She feels that you need to look at leadership through the eyes of your employees, and that what they are looking for is vision and a leader who lives up to their expectations, someone who 'walks the talk'.

It's no good thinking leadership is getting people to follow you. Bullshit! What you've got to do is shove them past you. My entire job is to motivate—and by that I mean show people a sense of their own power.[18]

Jannie Tay is another example of a successful woman entrepreneur who has found her own unique voice in developing her business. She began her career in a family business, but found their traditional, conservative approach to business too restricting. So she and her husband started in business for themselves, and she is now the Managing Director of The Hour Glass, a highly successful international organisation. She considers her employees to be her organisation's most important asset. There is a strong philosophy of customer service (and customers are considered to be internal just as much as external) and of fostering empowerment, communication, information sharing, teamwork and a close-knit family spirit among employees.[19]

Empowerment is a theme that is repeated over and over again by women leaders. Jannie Tay, for example, asserts that, 'To be able to function effectively, I believe that our front-line people must be empowered, given autonomy and trusted to do what they can do best.'[20] Mary Robinson put it like this at a conference on women and leadership which she hosted in Dublin in 1992: 'Women may well be establishing a new kind of leadership. One that does away with the traditional relationship between the individual and the group. One that is enabling and empowering of the individual and the group'.[21]

> 'If the best of me can make more of you then the best of you will reflect on me.'
> Natasha Josefowitz[22]

Grace M. Atkinson, Chairman, Hong Kong/China and an Executive Vice-President of J. Walter Thompson, has achieved a level in the business world of which few women even dream. Her approach to leadership is consistent with that of many other female leaders we have read about, listened to and spoken with.

. . . I pay attention to people in terms of training and motivation and how to instil a winning spirit in them. When I recognise good judgment and a good sense of value in a person . . . I give them opportunities. Usually they'll rise to the occasion. High profitability in an organisation is very important because it gives independence and autonomy. This way I can do more experimenting and be more creative in terms of client needs. I can also do more for the staff. And I can afford to attract the best people for the job.

My goal is to create a wholistic working environment where people are taken care of spiritually (I am cautious about using that word in business), mentally, physically and emotionally. I aim to treat all employees as internal customers. To all my managers I say 'Delegate to others and develop security in them and yourselves. You can only grow by becoming freer.'[23]

There is not yet an accepted leadership path for women to follow. At one level this is a handicap (where are the role models?) and yet at another level it is intensely liberating. Women are free to be and to become whatever they choose. And they have an added advantage because they don't need to unlearn old authoritarian behaviours to become responsive and effective leaders both today and into the future.

A different way of managing

The organisational structure set in place by the patriarchy was the hierarchy, a top-down approach typified diagrammatically by a pyramid. Power, control of information and decision making is vested at or near the top of the pyramid (see figure 10.1).

Rensis Likert describes the traditional organisation as following a 'man-to-man' pattern.[24] There is clearly no role for women leaders here. In this organisational structure there are well-defined areas of responsibility and chains of command. Information is power, and is seen as filtering up the organisation to the top. In practice, though, it is to the advantage of an individual manager to keep as much information as possible to himself. So he (and usually it will be 'he'

Figure 10.1   Traditional organisational structure

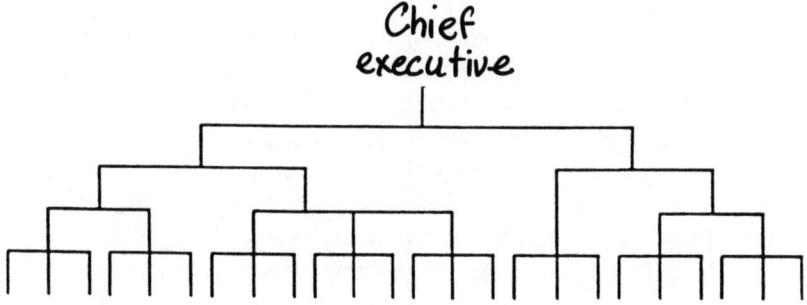

Chief
executive

in this organisational structure) tends to use his information selectively and in the interest of his own power and influence.

This attitude of self-interest rather than company interest tends to be a characteristic of the traditional organisation. Two and two always equal four and there is no real concept of synergy. There is a lack of understanding and interest in the problems, constraints and issues facing other departments. Instead there is fear, mistrust and competition between departments.

It is clear why it has been difficult for women to reach senior positions in the traditional organisation. They are excluded on all fronts—by the structure, the values, the basic premises and the actual methods of operation.

The natural female structure and ways of managing are very different. The closest analogy is that of the web.[25] A web is spun from the centre, with threads extending both out and across, all linked to the centre, to the heart of the web (see figure 10.2). This structure allows the female leader to operate in the way that is most natural to her—in the centre of things, rather than at the top.

In the web structure there is emphasis on a free flow of communication and information, a strong feeling of connection to all parts of the organisation, and a focus on building relationships and empowering others. While the leader remains ultimately accountable, individual responsibility, accountability and initiative are encouraged at all positions in the web. Status, hierarchy, rigid roles and formal channels of communication are de-emphasised, and

Figure 10.2   Web structure

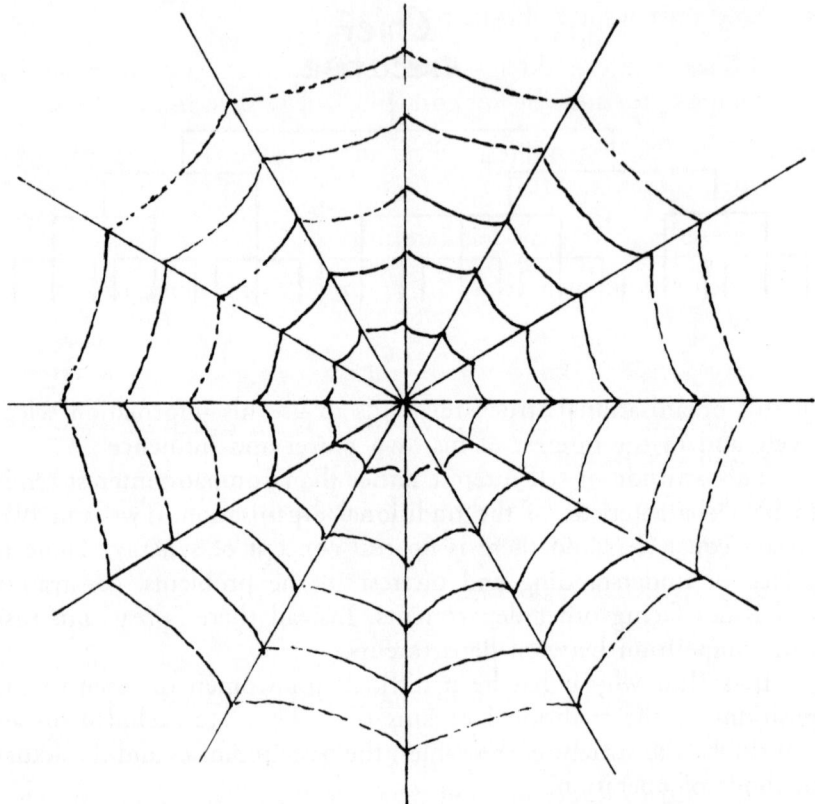

decisions can be taken at any point. Information can be gathered directly from its source. There is less opportunity, and less reason, for it to be filtered along the way.

The structure of the traditional organisation makes it slow to respond to change. While decisions are made at or near the top of the organisation and are dependent on the information that is filtered up, response to a new dynamic will always be sluggish. The web structure, with its open lines of communication and information gathering and its emphasis on relationships rather than status, is geared to adapt quickly to the incessant and turbulent changes brought about by the ending of the industrial age and the needs of the information age and beyond.

THE PATH TO LEADERSHIP

- You must want to do it, passionately.

- Believe you can do it—have confidence in your own ability, competence, and the support you will receive from others.

- Check that your values, beliefs and attitudes are supportive and empowering.

- Choose your role models carefully.

- Develop your own voice—be yourself, not a clone of someone else.

- Have a vision—know where you want to go.

- Be prepared to lead the way—to go first, to step in where you see an opportunity.

- Make sure you have support mechanisms in place—family, friends, colleagues, networks, coaches, mentors.

- Be prepared to take risks.

- Get noticed, become more visible.

- Be flexible, learn to ride the waves of change.

- Support and empower those around you.

- The path to leadership will take a lot of energy. Find out what you need to know about keeping fit—exercise and diet.

LEADERS OF THE FUTURE

Before information became available to humanity in abundance, government leaders and corporate chiefs were able to control the masses by withholding information. They controlled the key 'power card'—information. Now they can no longer do this; today's leaders and our future leaders will need to be more accountable, more driven by the needs of the people, more respectful, more wholistic in their thinking and decision making, more conscious of ethics and values and more able to lead in times of turmoil, rapid change and constant ambiguity.

Leadership of the future is bound to be different . . .

Leaders will be women as well as men. Each will learn from the other. Not only will we see traits of great leaders from the past but we will also witness a new kind of leadership—one that requires flexibility and creativity in rapidly changing and chaotic times. Men leaders will learn from women leaders and vice versa.

Our future leaders will

- have a knowing about what and how to do things. Where they don't, they'll learn from and accept the support of other leaders. They will be role models for each other as well as for their followers. Intuition and trust will be more commonly used terms.

- accept responsibility for their mistakes, learn from them and move on, wiser and often humbler from their learning experiences. Risk taking that produces beneficial results will be shared among others. So too will the learnings from unsuccessful attempts at taking risks.

- believe with a burning desire in their vision (dream) and, with their passion, be able to inspire others to reach for the same dream. Passionate leadership takes courage and courage comes from the heart, not the head.[26]

- demonstrate what they believe in by the actions they take, before they ask others to do the same. They will lead the way, and by going first they'll need to think about what they are demonstrating. 'Courage of their convictions' will take on even more meaning. For this reason, they'll make such great role models.

- empower others to take responsibility, to enjoy their work, to be creative, to grow, to accept visibility and power and to also lead.

- flow with the waves of change. The concepts of ambiguity and chaos will motivate and drive them to seek personal flexibility. Their example will encourage others to do the same.

- inspire others by communicating their dreams and their passions. All great leaders use their voice to communicate their vision.

IN SUMMARY

Leadership is the area where women can make a real difference—a difference to the values of organisations and the way they are run, a difference in our approach to the global economy, the environment and our fellow inhabitants on planet Earth.

> *'As women lead, they are changing leadership.*
> *As women organise, they are changing organisation.*
> *As they restate the skills of administration, of law,*
> *of the arts and the academy,*
> *women are handing them on*
> *in a fresh and radicalised form.'*
> Mary Robinson[27]

As we have seen, organisations are slowly changing in response to the needs of the information age and beyond. And this means that what we are looking for in a leader is also gradually changing. Organisations are being forced to rethink their traditional reverence for status, structure, top-down decision making and one's ability to play the 'game'. What is emerging is the need for open communication and information gathering, group involvement in decision-making processes and the ability to get things done by influencing and empowering people rather than through position power. And these are all natural female preferences.

There is another way of doing things—of running organisations, of leading at all levels and in all senses, of using resources, of living with each other, of providing for life on Earth now and into the future. Women with heart, who can focus on interdependence, nurturing and shared power, offer an alternative. Women are our hope for a brighter future . . .

11

BRIGHTNESS FOR
THE FUTURE!!

'Know the male,
Hold to the female,
Become the world's stream.'

The Tao of Power[1]

. . . BLAZING A NEW TRAIL

In the 1990s the global scene appears gloomy to many people. We have static or declining living standards in much of the world, chronic pollution, widespread devastation of the environment, wars and conflict, poverty, malnutrition and disease in underdeveloped countries. Do we want more of this as we move into the twenty-first century? And if our answer is 'no', what can we do to change the way things are?

Doing more of the same, producing more and more, is not the answer. We need to do something different in order to achieve different outcomes. And this is difficult for the people who benefit from the existing system. It is most likely that change will come from the groups who do not benefit from the patriarchal system and who will potentially gain from any move away from it. As David Suzuki says:

> . . . the people who today are offering vision and leadership come from groups that have traditionally been powerless and disenfranchised: the Third World, women, youth, elders, and indigenous people. . . . It is time for these disempowered groups to coalesce into an irresistible force for change on the planet.[2]

174

What do women offer?

The theme of this book is that women have a lot to offer. We are different from men and we do not have a commitment to the existing ways of doing business, running countries and relating to each other. We bring skills of cooperation, intuition, flexibility, sensitivity, patience, and willingness to share knowledge and experience. We have the ability to view things wholistically, and can imagine a different way of living and being. We can look for new solutions and new ways of doing things to create balance and harmony with the whole. We have the flexibility to decide what it is that we want, and then to become whatever we need to be in order to achieve that outcome. We have the capacity to lead the change and to create a new 'game' which offers a brighter future for nature and humankind. We understand that 'heart' is an important ingredient of successful business.

WHAT IS HOLDING WOMEN BACK?

So what has been stopping women? We are the majority of the world's population, so why are we not already playing a more influential role in business, politics and the environment?

A combination of genetic and hormonal factors, plus the reinforcing effect of conditioning, has led us to accept the world that has been created by patriarchal values and to try to make the best of things as they are. We are like the frog who stays in the saucepan while the temperature of the water is slowly raised. The frog doesn't attempt to jump out. She becomes accustomed to the gradual increases in temperature—until she cooks and dies. But by staying in the saucepan we are risking more than our individual lives. We are risking planet Earth and human life as we know it.

But it is more than this. The patriarchy itself has imposed boundaries on women. The occasional woman in a highly visible role has been tolerated, especially if she played the patriarchal 'game'. But the prospect of significant numbers of women in key positions is uncomfortable to those who support the conservative and inflexible values of the patriarchy.

Influential and highly visible women pose an unwanted challenge to the system. There is no guarantee that women who achieve positions of power and influence in substantial numbers will continue to play the 'game'. The silent 'minority' may well turn into an uncontrollable and highly vocal majority.

And women in leadership positions are also a threat to many other women. By moving into 'male' arenas, by questioning and challenging the rules and values of the patriarchy, they are disturbing existing patterns and threatening disharmony. There are still many women who feel that their place is in the home, that their most important roles are as supporters, carers and nurturers, and that pushing for women's rights and pursuing a career should be secondary considerations. There is still strong pressure on women to conform to the patriarchal picture. It is okay for them to go out to work to help support the family, but they should not look on their work as a career, try to move too far up the ladder, actively compete with men or disturb the status quo.

These factors are compelling, and help to explain why it has taken so long for women to reach influential positions in the world of business. Women have long been perceived, inaccurately, as a minority group. As such, it takes great strength of purpose and vision to make a difference.

Taking a minority stand

Pat O'Shane is a magistrate. She is a woman, which already makes her a minority in the male-dominated Australian judicial system. She is also an Aborigine, and an active defender of justice. She has made controversial decisions in favour of Aboriginal Australians which have alienated her from many police. Early in 1993 she handed down a decision and a public statement in favour of women which caused heated debate in the community.

In this case, since labelled the Berlei Billboard case, four women were charged with defacing a Berlei advertising billboard. On the billboard a young woman in underwear was lying prone, about to be sawn in half by a magician. The caption read: 'You'll always feel good in Berlei'. The women had added: 'Even if you're mutilated'.

Pat O'Shane dismissed the charges, and then went on to say:

> The real crime in this matter was the erection of these extremely offensive advertisements. . . . And what redress does 51 per cent of the population have? Absolutely none.

She was referring here to the dominance of male interests in controlling financial resources and in determining how we advertise. She then went even further:

> We have a very, very sorry society indeed when these women can be brought before this court for this sort of thing in the light of the depictions I find in the photograph of that particular advertisement. We live in a society where at least one and possibly more judicial officers can actually state to the world that the law will condone violence towards women. What sort of world are we creating for ourselves?[3]

Taking a strong minority stand in the patriarchal system needs conviction, commitment and, above all, bravery. Only a few strong people, like Pat O'Shane, will ever risk rocking the boat and alienating entrenched interests.

Women have an important contribution to make to our quality of life in the twenty-first century—if we choose to take the initiative. To do this, we must be willing to be different, to hold true to our deepest values, to risk hostility from entrenched attitudes, and to be prepared for and seek out leadership roles in every facet of life.

A 'BRIGHTNESS' SCENARIO

In the twenty-first century, women will make a difference in the values we hold and the way we do things at every level of human existence. Some women will choose to play in the business sphere, some in the political sphere, some in the realms of government, education, religion, the arts, sport, medicine and law. Others will choose the domestic sphere; it is their influence and their role modelling which will determine the values of future generations.

What is important is that we value the contributions made in each sphere equally.

Organisations are already being forced to change in response to the turbulence in their environments and markets. The organisation of the future will have a different shape and different values from the traditional organisation. We have talked about the emerging organisation, which incorporates more of the feminine values in its structure and operation. It is a flatter organisation, which has a focus on the centre, the resonant source, rather than the top. It emphasises and encourages creativity, communication, a free flow of information, networking, nurturing and the empowerment of others.

The future organisation will emphasise commitment, ethics, social and global responsibilities, and will value differences and the contribution of the individual. Words like 'love' and 'trust' and 'caring' will become more common in business. This type of organisation will have the capacity to think of the bigger picture. Not just the short-term bottom line, but the effects the organisation has on, and the contributions it can make to, other economies, the environment, other peoples and other living things.

The new organisation and the new way of doing things is an intuitively female way of operating. Women need to be there, in positions of power and influence, to show us how to do it—to pave the way for other women and to demonstrate to men how to manage and lead in the emerging organisation and the unknown world of the twenty-first century.

> *'Individual women are going to have to be willing to "go for it".'*
> Patricia Aburdene & John Naisbitt[4]

Some feel that we need to change from a male-dominated to a female-dominated system, from men on top to women on top. We see it differently. To us, brightness for the future is offered by a side-by-side, or hand-in-hand relationship, working together, recognising the differences between women and men, and valuing the contributions we can both bring to any situation. As Mary Robinson has said, 'I have a very strong view that it's not a question of making society more feminine. It's a question of making it more human through a better balance of the contribution of both sexes.'[5]

LIVING EXAMPLES OF 'BRIGHTNESS'

An example of 'brightness' is being played out on the world political stage with the partnership between Hillary and Bill Clinton. Bill is the President of the United States, and his wife Hillary is

> the first woman to arrive at the White House with a background equal to her husband's, an independent career as developed as his, and professional experience in policy activism on a par with his advisers. She is the first to have her own professional power base in Washington; the first whose only real disqualification from being a Cabinet member is the fact of being the president's wife.[6]

Theirs is a partnership of equals. Its mere existence at this level is both important and controversial because, as Gloria Steinem says, 'an equal relationship between a woman and a man is going against 5,000 years or more of patriarchy'.[7] Its perceived success or failure will determine what becomes possible for women in the future. Their partnership is different, controversial and threatening to many. It threatens to explode existing paradigms about the role of a wife as the quiet and supportive nurturer, and threatens the very nature of the 'game' of business and politics. If an equal relationship between a woman and a man works at the level of the US presidency, then the role model is established for such an equal partnership to work at any level of society, business or politics.

The example of Hillary and Bill is also interesting in that it represents a reversal of typical female and male characteristics. Bill is more intuitive, is anxious to please and is a slow decision maker. Hillary is seen as the strong partner. She is a rational thinker, makes decisions easily and has a forceful personality. Hillary's strength makes it okay for women to be seen as more assertive, competitive, rational and unemotional. A role model at Hillary's level is the strongest possible way to rapidly break down age-old stereotypes about female/male characteristics and roles.

Another example of 'brightness', this time in the world of

business, is provided by the partnership between Anita and Gordon Roddick. As Anita says:

> Many people perceive The Body Shop as a one-woman business. That's so far from the truth. It didn't even start that way— Gordon has always been involved from the very beginning. . . . Gordon and I operate on the partnership principle—he does his bit, and I do mine, but we do it together, with a common purpose . . .[8]

Anita and Gordon have different and complementary personalities and abilities. Anita refers to them as The Body Shop yin and yang. Their shared values are their great common bond. Gordon is quiet and introspective; he prefers a low profile. He gives to The Body Shop 'a sense of constancy and continuity' and is 'well known to everyone, much loved and deeply respected as the real strength of the company'.[9] On the other hand, Anita sees herself as loud and brash, bouncing about 'breaking the rules, pushing back the boundaries of possibility and shooting off my mouth'.[10] She is the mouth piece of the company, and Gordon makes it happen.

Robert Kiyosaki, American business man and global educator, has also experienced the 'brightness' we are talking about in his business relationships.

In 1985 I formed my first company with two equal women partners. Until then, I only had men as partners. Had I known how much better, easier and more profitable business would be with women as partners I would have done it years ago. While it took time to adjust to a woman's way of doing business, and although there were some heated arguments on handling certain problems, I discovered some very interesting things.

For me women partners produced two outcomes I did not always have with men—peace and profitability. Once we had peace and profitability I did not care about my great business mind or who was which sex. Peace and profitability are much better than ego and debt. I know my experience is limited and maybe I got lucky—but I would venture to say that women are better at business than men . . .

I found that women often work more diligently than men, handle problems and people with greater compassion, are better with money and think long-term in business. When I finally allowed women to be equal I found I could use my often volatile male tendencies to more productive, rather than destructive ends. A gift I have received from women is that I am able to speak with kindness and compassion to people, even when I am angry with them. That ability has brought people closer instead of blowing the business apart. Not only have my relationships with women improved, my relationships with men are now kinder and much less filled with ego-driven superficiality. When there is peace, trust and love, profits often follow.[11]

WHAT ABOUT THE FAMILY?

Will women have to sacrifice other areas of their lives to achieve success in a career? The potential conflict between the needs of a family and the demands of a career has always been a 'catch 22' for women. The newer breed of women executives and entrepreneurs believe that women can have it all—career, marriage, children and supportive friendships. According to Jannie Tay:

> You just have to be very focused on your goals and work towards them. Try to figure out in your mind and understand that the three key factors in your life are your career or business, your family and your husband. Prioritize these three objectives and you certainly can have it all![12]

Jannie is a living example of this, as she is the managing director of a successful publicly-listed organisation with outlets in Singapore, Kuala Lumpur, Jakarta and Australia, a wife and a mother to three children.

And society must also look at its values. Humankind needs children. We do so much in the name of 'providing for future generations'. But families are not the responsibility of women alone; they are the responsibility of women and men. And yet it tends to be women who care for children, the sick and the elderly. As we saw in chapter 4, caring and nurturing are natural female tendencies which are heavily reinforced by conditioning. Women feel responsible for the well-being of their families, and guilty and negligent if there are problems. While more men are helping with family and domestic tasks than ever before, these issues will never be addressed properly until they are recognised as being the responsibility, not just of women, but of society. Meredith Hellicar puts it this way:

> The solution is convincing men that they've got to share the responsibility for, not just the doing of, home duties, and society's expectations are going to have to change to allow men to take on this responsibility.[13]

As it is, the rules are not the same for all women. How could the Queen of England have her children brought up by nannies, while she continued in a full-time job?[14] How have the wealthy worldwide always been able to do this? Why should the rules be different for some women? It is only our conditioning which, until recently, has made it unacceptable for other wives and mothers to continue to work full time if they chose to.

In Europe, the UK and the US, new ways of working are already emerging that make it easier for women and men to combine parenthood (or eldercare) with a career. The electronic village is a reality,[15] as are increasing numbers of small specialist businesses which service larger organisations. Working flexible hours and working from home both provide more opportunities for people to approach their lives wholistically.

Even in traditional organisations, as the contribution of women in the workforce is increasingly valued, our attitudes to childcare are changing. Childcare facilities are gradually being seen as something that must be offered by organisations if they want to attract the most able employees.

Men, and society generally, are not going to change voluntarily. Even though it has many negative precessional effects, the patriarchal system is comfortable for most men. As we keep emphasising in this book, the driving force for change must come from groups, such as women, who are disadvantaged by the existing system. If we don't like the way things are now, then we must do something about it. And every individual, each one of us, can make a difference by our actions.

PLAYING OUTSIDE THE BOX[16]

How can you do something different, so that you can make a difference?

- **Question everything**

  Don't take anything for granted, or assume that it's okay because others say so.

  Is the education system giving your children what they need? Are they learning vital life skills so that they can cope in the changing years ahead?

  Are we valuing and using the experience, knowledge and wisdom of the elders in our society? Older people have a wealth of knowledge and experience and time for caring which is utilised to the benefit of all in primitive societies, but which we, in so-called developed economies, throw away.

  Why can't women hold key executive positions and raise children at the same time? What kind of system will make this possible?

- **Develop curiosity**

  . . . just like a little child. The more you ask, the more you will notice the reactions of others.

  Are they defensive? Ask yourself why?

  Don't they want to give you answers? Why?

  Brainstorm with your work team. Look for new possibilities, new ways of working with people, different ways of looking at things.

  What if things were done differently? What effect would this have? Explore what works, as well as what doesn't work.

- **Daydream**

  . . . of how the world can be and how your life can be.

  Imagine yourself 50 years from now looking back on how things have changed in the world.

  How has the world become a better place because differences are valued and women and men work alongside each other?

  What are the precessional effects?

  Is the planet in better shape since we have once again learnt to live cooperatively with mother Earth?

- **Seek new possibilities**

  Think outside the box. Look for new ways of seeing, feeling, hearing, saying and doing.

  What role can you foresee for men in the new brightness?

  Put yourself in the shoes of men. How would you feel if your foundations and security were being rocked?

  What will it look like when women and men truly work together, valuing the contributions that each can make?

  Will it feel more or less comfortable for you to work and live this way?

  What effect will this new way of being have on the human race, on business, on our attitude to crime, to war, to the environment, to solving problems and conflicts?

- **Try new things**

  Replay the messages of your childhood.

  Is what you say to yourself, your internal dialogue, supportive or limiting?

  Will it allow your true purpose to be fulfilled?

  If not, consciously erase any self-talk or messages that are limiting.

  Also become aware of your values, beliefs and attitudes.

Are they supporting you in creating the future that you want?

What do you need to do to change limiting values, beliefs and attitudes to empowering ones?

Actively seek knowledge and new learnings—in books, at seminars and workshops and through role models, coaches and guides.

What effect will doing this have on your partner, on your family, your friends and your career?

Nurture yourself. Investigate and experiment with diet, exercise, body work, self-help and alternative therapies.

- **Take risks**

Be willing to put yourself on the line and keep stretching your comfort zone.

Take one step at a time.

Use your intuition and knowing to guide you into creating the brightest future you can imagine for yourself.

Don't let what others say or think stop you from getting what you deserve.

Be a pioneer.[17]

Just as women in the workforce were pioneers in the 1970s and 1980s, so female leaders are pioneers in the 1990s and beyond. They
- take risks
- break new ground
- venture into new territory
- act without full knowledge of where they are headed or the challenges that lie ahead
- are highly individualistic, but depend on their team for success
- empower others to be whatever they choose to be
- rely on their own core values

- **Actively encourage role modelling and mentoring**

Join a new group or network and develop new interests.

Support others to be the best they can be, pick them up when they are down, dust them off and encourage them to keep moving and learning.

Be willing to have others see you as a role model. Accept the role with responsibility and humility.

Demonstrate your commitment to making this a better planet for all of humanity.

Speak out about valuing differences—because in speaking out we will enhance the existence of today's many so-called minority groups.

- **Create new waves**

  Get on the crest of a wave, look over the top and bingo—go off on a wave of your own!

  A new wave is a new game—a new way of doing things and seeing things.

  How can you best contribute to a game that values differences in cultures, religions, races and genders?

IN SUMMARY

Despite the popular perceptions that women are a minority group and the 'weaker' sex, we are in fact statistically a majority. Right now, we are on the threshhold of change. Naomi Wolf[18] calls it an 'open moment' for the female race. This is our opportunity to speak out, to stand up and celebrate our majority status. To make this 'open moment' a victory for women and a defeat for men is, in our view, a mistake. For while we are different, we are not separate from men. Each of us has a male, as well as a female, side within us. In the same way, every man has a female, as well as a male, side. We must utilise the strength of our majority status to ensure that both women and men value the complementary contributions each can make and celebrate our differences and uniqueness.

It is up to women with voice, in cooperation with willing men, to dispel the notion of difference as an anomaly, an inefficient equation, and to broadcast the amazing power and synergy of difference that is directed towards a common objective.

Buckminster Fuller, humanity's friendly genius, had a saying: 'Unity is plural and at minimum two'.[19]

It's time to unify as women. To support each other in being the best that we can be in whatever area we as individuals choose.

It's time to unify with men. By valuing the different contributions that each of us make we can together create a world far beyond what we have experienced until now.

It's time to unify with mother Earth. So that life on Earth can be sustained for our children and our children's children and all other living things, infinitely into the future.

We have come a long way and now the opportunities for positive change are within our grasp. The brightness for the future rests with women who are prepared to work together with men to create a new and positive future for the human race and planet Earth. Nothing is more important than this.

We must speak out and live our support for a more caring, a more effective way of living, communicating and working. This book is our way of saying why and how.

EXERCISES

CHAPTER 2 FOR THINGS TO CHANGE . . .

How to identify and rank your values

Here is a simple exercise to help you identify and rank your own values.[1]

Step I
First of all, focus on what's important to you in your personal life. Let your mind run free and write down as many words as possible on a sheet of paper. You may choose to use different colours in this exercise. It's important to let your thoughts flow freely and not to censor or judge any of the words you are writing down.

This process can be time constrained; for example, you can set a limit of 10 minutes for doing the exercise. Or, you can do it over a number of days, writing down values as they occur to you.

This exercise is going to be most useful for you if you focus your brain precisely on things that are important to you in your life. Keep asking yourself the question:

What's important to me, personally, in my life?

Step 2

Once you have written as many value words as you can think of, highlight or circle the ones that jump out at you as being the most important.

Now, write these on a piece of paper like:

_____	_____	_____	_____
_____	_____	_____	_____
_____	_____	_____	_____

You may find maybe six or even twenty words jump out at you; either is okay.

Step 3

Next, rank the values in order of importance to you. To do this, take the word that you feel is the most important and ask yourself, as a check, if it is more important to you than each of the other values you have listed. Continue this with each value until you have them ranked in order of importance.

For example, assume that your list of values includes the following:

love   enjoyment   respect   freedom
security   family   wealth

You think that the most important of these values to you is **freedom**, so now you check it against the others by asking yourself, 'Is **freedom** more important to me than **enjoyment**?' and so on through the list of words.

There are two things that can happen. One is that you realise that **freedom** is definitely more important to you than each of the other values. The other is that one or two of the other words start to become more important than **freedom**. In this case go through the checklist again, asking yourself if one is more important than any of the other values until you determine the one that is most important to you.

Repeat this process with all the words. What you will end up with is a list of values in hierarchical order that relate to your personal life at this moment in time.

Step 4

Now, identify and rank your values (steps 1 to 3) in the context of your worklife. Ask yourself the question:

'What's important to me about my job/career?'

How to change your values

What we do and the actions we take determine what results we get in life. One of the ways we can change the results we get is by changing one or more of our values. So, if you don't like what's showing up in your life, then a first step is to look at your values.

There are potentially three aspects of your values that you may like to look at in terms of their usefulness to you:

- adding new values to your existing hierarchy
- changing the order of your values
- taking values out of your hierarchy

Here is a simple strategy for changing the order of your values, or adding in new values.[2]

How it works is . . .

Go back to your hierarchy of values list, where you ranked your values in order of importance to you.

*Now let's say that your number one work value is **achievement** and that another value, although ranked much lower, is **money**. As a result of this ranking you tend to achieve what you want but you don't get paid the money you would like. So you've decided that you'd like to rank **money** higher on your list of values, because by doing this you'll alter your behaviour in such a way that will allow you to earn more.*

*The next thing to do is to notice everything about how you represent to yourself your number one value of **achievement**.*

How do you know when your value has been attained? How do you know when you have achieved? Do you hear others acknowledging you or do you acknowledge yourself in words, using internal dialogue (auditory)? Does the pat on the back and feeling of satisfaction come from external sources or from within (kinaesthetic)? Or do you repre-sent achievement in the form of pictures in colour or black and white (visual)? [3]

Become aware of how you represent achievement to yourself and whether your first preference is visual, auditory or kinaesthetic (touch and emotion). The way you represent your top value can be duplicated exactly on to another value. In other words, by discovering the precise way you represent a value (using as many of the senses as possible), you can then in your own mind start representing the value you want to change in exactly the same way. The idea being, that whatever you are doing with your number one value to get the results you want, this same strategy can be transferred to a value of lesser importance.

In this way you can move a lesser ranked value higher up on your ranking of values. Once it's higher it becomes more important to you and your actions and behaviours start reflecting this importance. The result, in the context of this example, means more money.

You can also use exactly the same strategy to introduce a new value to your hierarchy of values.

To really grasp this skill, you might need to practise it over and over, either alone or with someone else. [4]

CHAPTER 3 SELF-FULFILLING PROPHECIES

V-B-A chain

The differences between values, beliefs and attitudes may be confusing at times. To gain finer distinctions on your V-B-As refer to page 41 and try this exercise.

Using the information you now have about values, beliefs and attitudes, construct three empowering V-B-A chains for yourself. Make sure that at least one chain is focused on your career and at least one is focused on your family/personal life.

CHAPTER 5 GENDER TALK . . .

Matching the behaviour of others

Try this exercise with a family member or a friend to start with.

Carefully observe as many distinctive things about their physiology as you can. Use the mind map on matching (figure 5.2 on page 72) as a check list. Begin with one part of their body—something noticeable and fairly easy to match.

Then match more of their behaviours. Speak at the same tempo and at a similar pitch as them, sit or stand or move the same way, breathe in the same pattern as they do, and so on.

After you have been matching behaviours for a couple of minutes, ask them how they feel. Chances are they'll feel very close to you.

Use this technique with strangers and they may start talking to you! Once you feel comfortable with this technique, try it in the work environment—it really works!

What is your preferred sensory system?[5]

Part I

For each item below, circle the response that most closely describes your typical behaviour. Do this exercise quickly.

1. *In a meeting, I tend to . . .*
   A. *take lots of notes, often with lots of doodles*
   B. *sit near the action so I can hear and participate in discussions*
   C. *get restless quickly, have the urge to move around*

2. *I get the most out of workshops where the presenter . . .*
   A. *is a good speaker*
   B. *uses lots of audio-visual aids and handouts*
   C. *involves participants in exercises and hands-on experiences*

3. *When someone asks me to critique something they have written, I prefer to . . .*
   A. *read it aloud while pacing about*
   B. *read it quietly to myself*
   C. *have it read to me*

4. When I need to make a big decision, I prefer to . . .
   A. sit in a comfortable place and listen to music
   B. analyse my options on paper
   C. do something active like jogging, walking, or working in the garden

5. When I study a foreign language, I prefer to . . .
   A. try the language out in real life situations
   B. speak the language in the classroom
   C. read and write the language

6. Before buying a major item, such as a car, I prefer to . . .
   A. get as much written information on the item as I can
   B. talk to friends and associates for their advice
   C. try the item out or see it in person

7. When learning how to use a new piece of equipment, I prefer to . . .
   A. have someone tell me how to get started
   B. read all the directions before trying it out
   C. set it up and try it out first

8. When I get angry, I tend to . . .
   A. clench my fists, pound the table, storm off
   B. clam up and keep it to myself
   C. quickly let others know I am angry

9. In my spare time, I prefer to . . .
   A. watch TV, go to the movies, go to a play, or read
   B. engage in a physical activity
   C. listen to the radio, play music, or go to a concert

Part 2

Each question includes three lists of words. Circle the list—A, B or C—that is easiest for you to read. Work quickly, and do not focus on the meanings of the words.

10. A. witness   B. interview   C. sensation
       look   listen   touch
       see   hear   feel

11. A. *stir* B. *watch* C. *squeal*
    sensitive   *scope*   *remark*
    hustle   *pinpoint*   *discuss*

12. A. *dream* B. *listen* C. *motion*
    glow   *quiet*   *soft*
    illusion   *silence*   *tender*

13. A. *upbeat* B. *firm* C. *bright*
    listen   *hold*   *appear*
    record   *concrete*   *picture*

14. A. *feeling* B. *hindsight* C. *hearsay*
    lukewarm   *purple*   *audible*
    muscle   *book*   *horn*

Part 3

This part consists of five sets of three short phrases. In each question, circle the letter (A, B or C) of the phrase that you find easiest to read.

15. A. *Lend me an ear* B. *Give her a hand* C. *Keep an eye out*

16. A. *Get the picture* B. *Hear the word* C. *Come to grips with*

17. A. *Thrill of the chase* B. *A flash of lightning* C. *The roll of thunder*

18. A. *Hang in there* B. *Bird's eye view* C. *Rings true*

19. A. *Clear as a bell* B. *Smooth as silk* C. *Bright as day*

Preferred sensory system—response sheet

Transfer your responses to this sheet by circling the letter that you chose for each of the numbered items in the questionnaire, then total your responses in each column.

		Auditory	Visual	Kinaesthetic
Part I	1.	B	A	C
	2.	A	B	C
	3.	C	B	A
	4.	A	B	C
	5.	B	C	A
	6.	B	A	C
	7.	A	B	C
	8.	C	B	A
	9.	C	A	B
Part 2	10.	B	A	C
	11.	C	B	A
	12.	B	A	C
	13.	A	C	B
	14.	C	B	A
Part 3	15.	A	C	B
	16.	B	A	C
	17.	C	B	A
	18.	C	B	A
	19.	A	C	B
Total		____	____	____

CHAPTER 6 DOING IT DIFFERENTLY . . .

Brain dominance questionnaire[6]

Quickly circle the most accurate answer:

1. Do you lose track of time:
   A. often
   B. occasionally
   C. rarely

2. If playing a musical instrument would you:
   A. prefer to play by ear
   B. read sheet music
   C. have no preference

3. When reading books for pleasure, are they:
   A. most likely non-fiction
   B. fiction and non-fiction
   C. most likely fiction

4. Do you follow gut feelings or hunches:
   A. rarely
   B. often
   C. sometimes

5. During your latter days of schooling did you mainly study:
   A. science
   B. humanities
   C. commerce

6. With regard to maths, do you prefer:
   A. algebra
   B. geometry
   C. no preference

7. Do you persuade with:
   A. facts and figures
   B. appeals to emotion
   C. both

8. Are your pastimes likely to be:
   A. competitive
   B. non-competitive
   C. both

9. Do your moods change:
   A. frequently
   B. occasionally
   C. rarely

10. If learning a song, which would you learn faster?
    A. the music
    B. the words
    C. neither

11. Do you believe you could be hypnotised?
    A. with difficulty
    B. easily
    C. not at all

12. Is your personal workplace:
    A. fairly tidy all the time
    B. more often messy than tidy
    C. more often tidy than messy

13. Do you find yourself humming songs or jingles:
    A. often
    B. occasionally
    C. never

14. Would you say you daydream:
    A. rarely
    B. occasionally
    C. never

15. When taking notes, do you:
    A. print
    B. write
    C. equally

16. Are you:
    A. right-handed
    B. left-handed
    C. both equally

17. In meetings would you:
    A. take lots of notes
    B. take few notes
    C. both according to need

18. Clasp both hands together. Notice where your thumb is:
   A. right on top
   B. left on top
   C. side by side

19. Look at a distant object along your forefinger. Now close your right eye:
   A. the object still aligns with your finger
   B. it no longer aligns

20. Are you more:
   A. logical and analytical
   B. imaginative and intuitive

Brain dominance—response monitor

Legend:

L = left
R = right
N = neutral

	A.	B.	C.
1.	R	N	L
2.	L	R	N
3.	L	N	R
4.	L	R	N
5.	L	R	N
6.	N	L	R
7.	L	R	N
8.	L	R	N
9.	R	N	L
10.	R	L	N
11.	N	L	R
12.	N	R	L
13.	R	N	L
14.	N	R	L
15.	R	L	N
16.	L	N	R
17.	L	N	R
18.	L	R	N
19.	R	L	
20.	L	R	

Total your L (left brain) and R (right brain) responses.

Accessing the right brain

The right brain is uninhibited, spontaneous and random. To engage it we need to put ourselves into a playful, open, trusting state. For some, this might be a real stretch, so here is a useful way in:

Remember a time when you felt playful, open and trusting.
Go back to that time and imagine yourself there now.

What are you

seeing?
hearing?
feeling?
intuiting?

Be very specific and recreate the state as closely as possible.

Perhaps you have not felt like this since you were a child. For some of us, it is quite a regular experience!

With this new awareness, notice, from now on, the times when you are naturally in a right brain state.

How and why are you choosing to access your right hemisphere?

Next time you have to tackle a creative task or make a major decision, consciously call on your right hemisphere. Notice any differences in your effectiveness and the end result.

CHAPTER 7 CREATING YOUR FUTURE . . .

Visioning

Put yourself into a right brain state (see p. 200).

Fantasise or day dream about your career.

What is your vision for your future?

It is often useful to look well into the future and work backwards towards the present. Where would you like to be, and what would you like to be doing, in

10 years' time?
3 years?
1 year?

What do you need to be, to do and to have in order to fulfil the dreams of your future?

Anchoring

Step 1

Think of a time when you were successful. Perhaps when you first rode a bike without falling off, when you won an important race or clinched a big sale or contract, passed a vital examination or achieved a promotion you had worked hard for.

Imagine yourself there now.

What are you seeing around you? Who are the people? Where are you precisely? Are you inside or outside? Is it day or night? What are the colours in your environment?

Listen to the sounds.

What are you hearing precisely? Are people talking or is there silence? What are you saying to yourself? Are there sounds of anything else around you, such as music or birds or machinery?

Get in touch with your feelings.

What emotions are you experiencing? Is your body involved in any kind of activity? What are you doing with your hands? Are you sitting, *standing or lying down? Are your eyes open or closed? What are you wearing?*

As precisely and as intensely as possible, recreate your successful time.

Step 2

When you are fully associated with the experience, imagine a circle on the floor in front of you. If it helps, colour the circle and, if necessary, actually draw a circle on the floor. Do whatever you need to do to make the exercise as real as possible.

Step 3

While deeply associated to your successful experience take a deep breath and step into the circle. For most people, when first using this strategy, it works best to step physically into an imagined circle. If it's neither appropriate nor comfortable to do this, then it's okay to imagine it without having to actually move.

Step 4

Stand inside the circle and intensify your memory as if it is happening now. This is one way of anchoring to a successful time in your life. To reinforce the experience you can also set other anchors, such as:

- *for kinaesthetics—take your thumb and forefinger and lightly squeeze your ear lobe at the height of your recreated successful experience. Other ways are to make a fist or take a deep breath.*

- *for auditories—use a code word and say it aloud or to yourself at the height of the recreated experience. For example say the word 'yes' or 'success'.*

- *for visuals—the circle, particularly in lots of colour, and the recreated imagined experience is probably enough.*

CHAPTER 8 FAST TRACKING TO SUCCESS . . .

Choosing mentors and role models

If you want to work on choosing mentors and role models try this exercise. You might find it useful to work on one at a time. If your role model is accessible then spend as much time as you can with them—pick their brains and find out specifically what makes them tick! If they are not accessible then read as much as you can about them and watch videos or live footage, if available. Also think about the mentors and role models that have worked for you in the past . . .

Spend a few minutes identifying significant past and present mentors and role models in your life. Write them down.

Are they male or female?

Which of these has influenced your behaviour, values, beliefs and attitudes or changed your life in some way?

Did you choose this influence consciously or unconsciously?

Knowing what you know now, would you consciously choose the same models again?

Develop and write out an action plan. Be as specific as possible. Ask yourself questions such as:

- *Who specifically?*

- *How specifically?*

- *When? By when?*

- *Why?*

- *What specifically? What if?*

- *Where does this apply?*

State your plan in the positive, present tense and active voice. For example: 'I am successfully modelling Whoopi Goldberg's sense of humour which is poignant, honest and to the point. The fact that she puts the message into a humorous context takes some of the sharpness away. I am finding this very useful in relating certain things that would otherwise seem very serious.'

When consciously choosing a role model and mentor consider the attributes that you desire in order to produce the results that you want, such as: age, skills, profession, organisation, female/male, desirable traits, values and beliefs (e.g. trustworthy, caring).

Also include in your plan the likely places and networks for sourcing the people who will assist you the most. Will it be through:

- *professional associations?*
- *community groups?*
- *special interest groups?*
- *sporting or other clubs?*
- *groups of family relatives and friends?*
- *social contacts and acquaintances?*
- *work—current and past colleagues?*
- *conferences, seminars, training courses?*

How will you know when you have achieved your outcome? Again be very specific and include what you will be:

- *seeing*

- *hearing*

- *feeling*

CHAPTER 9 BEYOND THE COMFORT ZONE . . .

Extending your comfort zone

What stops you from stepping beyond the comfort zone? Is it because you have been conditioned to play it safe or have taken risks that didn't work out?

These exercises can help you make informed choices about taking risks and stretching beyond your comfort zone:

- *Revisit your own values, beliefs and attitudes.*

- *Divide them into acceptors and resistors (refer to page 146 for more details).*

- *Are your values and beliefs encouraging or discouraging you from taking risks?*

- *Make a conscious choice to add at least one new acceptor strategy to your behaviour.*

- *Examine your own comfort zone. How long is it since you stretched your boundaries? Think of an activity that would be a real stretch for you (e.g., joining a new group, trying out a new sport, learning a new skill). Do it.*

- *Afterwards, acknowledge yourself and consciously anchor success to stretching your comfort zone (see chapter 7 on anchoring to success). Consciously expand your comfort zone on a regular basis.*

- *Think of a decision that you made in the past which had unforeseen negative results. In hindsight what have you learned from the experience? Were there any positive precessional effects? On balance, was the 'mistake' a positive learning experience for you? Would you make the same decision again?*

CHAPTER 10 WALKING THE TALK . . .

Power

Here is an exercise around the word 'power'.

Think about the word 'power' for a few minutes and refer to the figure below. Consider the circle of power in terms of how you use, and see others using power.

1. *What is your perception of power? What has been your experience of power in your working life as well as in your personal life? Have your experiences been negative or positive?*

Figure 10.3

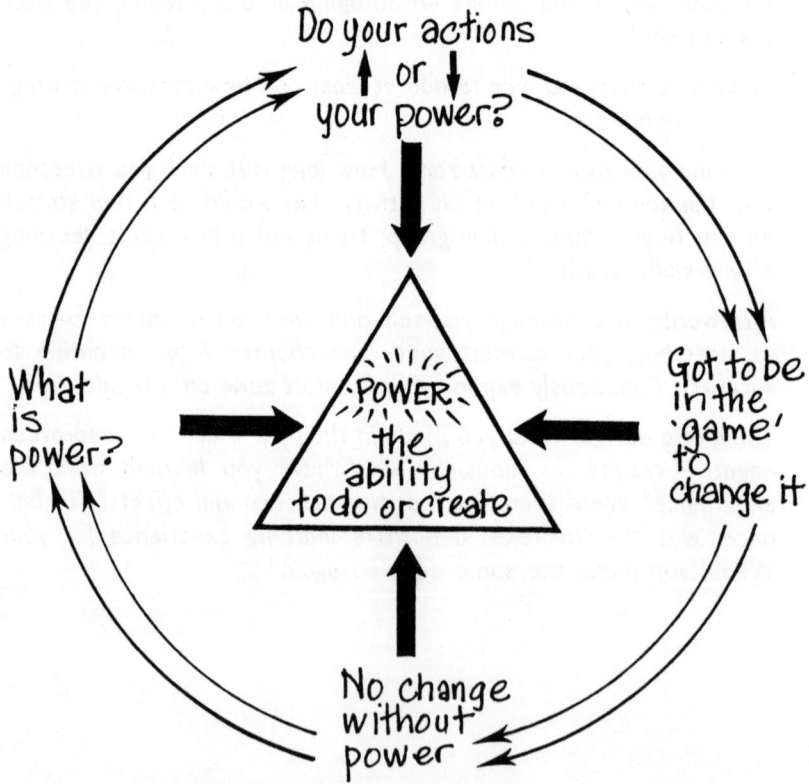

Source: Originally created for K. Chater & R. Gaster, *Trainers Guide to 'Breakthrough: Beyond the Glass Ceiling' (video)*

2. Do your actions increase or decrease your ability to do, act or create? What about the actions of others—do they assist you or hamper you? What can you do to increase your own personal power?

3. With the definitions of power—the ability to do or create—in mind, what can you personally do, what actions can you take, to bring about a change in the game? Are you playing at sufficient levels in order to be able to effect change in the game?

4. There can be no change without power—without action and doing. Negative change can occur just as easily as positive change. How do you contribute to making a positive change?

NOTES

CHAPTER I LIVING IN A PATRIARCHY . . .

1 Quote from Sally Helgesen, *The Female Advantage*, Doubleday Currency, New York, 1990, p. xxi.
2 Quote from UNICEF diary 1993, UNICEF Committee of Australia.
3 Interview with Carolyn Brand on 15 June 1992. Used with permission. At the time of the interview, Carolyn Brand was the Commanding Officer of HMAS *Waterhen*, the mine warfare headquarters base for the Royal Australian Navy.
4 Statistics sourced from Natasha Josefowitz, *Paths to Power*, Addison Wesley, Reading, Massachusetts, 1980, p. 195; *Half Way to Equal*, Report into Equal Opportunity and Equal Status for Women in Australia, Australian Government Publishing Service, Canberra, 1992, pp. 51 and 165; John Naisbitt and Patricia Aburdene, *Megatrends 2000*, William Morrow and Company, New York, 1990, pp. 217 and 226; *Sunday Times*, London, 14 February 1993; the United Nations as quoted in 'Not a Bedroom War', SBS-TV, Anne Deveson Productions, Sydney, 1993.
5 Video on WOW'M, Women of the World Mentoring, 1993, Verna Salmon and Amy Burgess, founders of Women of the World Mentoring.

6 Quote from Anne Summers, *Damned Whores and God's Police*, Penguin Books Ltd, Australia, 1975, p. 467.

7 Quote from Naomi Wolf, *Fire with Fire*, Chatto & Windus, London, 1993, p. 57.

8 A negative future scenario for the world is spelled out by Eugene Linden in 'Too Many People', American *Time* Magazine, Fall 1992.

9 Susan Faludi, *Backlash: The Undeclared War Against Women*, Chatto & Windus, London, 1992; Marilyn French, *The War Against Women*, Hamish Hamilton, London 1992; and Naomi Wolf, *The Beauty Myth*, Vintage, London, 1990, all discuss different aspects of the backlash.

10 Definition of a game first heard in a workshop led by Robert Kiyosaki of the Excellerated Learning Institute (ELI), an international education company committed to applying leading edge training methodologies and the principles of accelerated learning to enhance the performance of both individuals and corporations.

11 Quote from Robert Kiyosaki, *If You Want to Be Rich and Happy . . . Don't Go to School*, Excellerated Learning Publishing, California, 1991, p. 106.

12 Joel A. Barker, *Discovering the Future: the Business of Paradigms*, I. L. I. Press, St Paul, Minnesota, 1989, p. 119–20.

13 Quote from John Naisbitt and Patricia Aburdene, op. cit., p. 235. The ideas and research of these authors have crystallised many of our ideas and thinking about the potential of women in the world of business.

CHAPTER 2 FOR THINGS TO CHANGE . . .

1 Quote by Lao Tsu from R. L. Wing (ed.), *The Tao of Power*, Aquarian/Thomsons, London, 1986, Number 33.

2 Values development stages taken from Tad James and Wyatt Woodsmall, *Time Line Therapy and the Basis of Personality*, Meta Publications, California, US, 1988, chapter 17, and Gail Sheehy, *Passages*, Bantam Books in association with E. P. Dutton, New York, 1976.

3 It should be noted that Morris Massey's three major periods of values and personality development are not universally accepted. In particular, it is often held that a fourth period, from 22 to 29 years, is also critical to our values formation.

4 At a deeper level, some fascinating work on the idea of the evolution of values over time was done by Dr Claire Graves. An introduction

to Graves's system of values is given in Tad James and Wyatt Woodsmall, *Time Line Therapy and the Basis of Personality*, op. cit., chapter 18.

5 Quote from Anthony Robbins, *Unlimited Power*, Simon and Schuster, New York, 1986, p. 301.

6 Story taken from Anita Roddick's book *Body and Soul*, Ebury Press, London, 1991, chapter 1. Anita's descriptions of her unconventional and highly successful entry into the world of big business are an inspiring validation that the intuitive female approach can and does work.

7 Charles Handy, *The Age of Unreason*, Arrow Books, London, 1989, chapter 4.

8 A lot of attention has been focused on the glass ceiling recently. For example, Women & Management in Sydney produced a video in 1991 entitled 'Breakthrough: Beyond the Glass Ceiling', which looked at strategies to help women move more readily into senior management positions.

9 We give examples of women's networks and other support mechanisms in chapter 8.

10 Knocking down the tall poppies, or putting down people who achieve above their peers, seems to be peculiar to the Australian and New Zealand cultures.

11 Statistics on women in small business from John Naisbitt and Patricia Aburdene, *Megatrends 2000*, William Morrow and Company, New York, 1990, p. 226 and Kate Lyons 'Women in Bu$iness', *Australian Small Business and Investing*, July 1992.

12 At an unconscious level, women have a complementary masculine element, and men a complementary feminine element. Carl Jung called these the animus and the anima, respectively.

CHAPTER 3 SELF-FULFILLING PROPHECIES . . .

1 Paraphrased from Anthony Robbins, *Unlimited Power*, Simon and Schuster, New York, 1986, p. 64.

2 Sources of beliefs adapted from Anthony Robbins, *Unlimited Power*, op. cit., chapter 4.

3 Quote from Learning to Learn seminar, developed by Stephanie Burns. This powerful workshop utilises leading edge training methodologies, including accelerated learning.

4 Leonie Still, *Everything a Woman Needs to Know About Winning the Corporate Battle*, Horwitz Grahame, Sydney, 1986, p. 47.

5 Quote from Natasha Josefowitz, *Paths to Power*, Addison Wesley, Reading, Massachusetts, 1980, p. 61, a book about how women can succeed in organisations.

6 Conversation with Lana Syriatowicz, Sydney architect, on 12 November 1992. Used with permission.

7 Simone de Beauvoir, *The Second Sex*, Penguin Books, England, 1975.

8 Adele Horin, 'Why middle-class men no longer marry down', *Sydney Morning Herald*, 17 November 1992, p. 14.

9 In fact, the majority of women continue to be in low income, low status jobs.

10 Martin Jacques 'His, and hers', the *Sunday Times*, London, 14 February 1993.

11 Interview with Grace M. Atkinson on 8 December 1992. Used with permission.

CHAPTER 4 BRAIN SEX . . .

1 Quote from Natasha Josefowitz, *Paths To Power*, Addison Wesley, Reading, Massachusetts, 1980, p. 2. Used with permission.

2 Interview with Carolyn Brand on 15 June 1992. Used with permission.

3 Quote from Philip Zimbardo, 'Sex and Gender', Discovering Psychology series, a documentary screened on SBS-TV, Sydney, 1992, focusing on the differences between the genders.

4 Quote from Anne Moir and David Jessel, *Brain Sex*, Mandarin Paperback, London, 1989, p. 182.

5 Quote from Christine Gorman, 'Sizing up the sexes', *Time* Australia, 20 January 1992, p. 30.

6 This section owes much to 'Sex and Gender', Discovering Psychology series, a documentary screened on SBS-TV, Sydney, 1992; Anne Moir and David Jessel's *Brain Sex*, op. cit., which is based on research into sex differences; the TV series 'Brain Sex', 1993, Primedia Productions Limited, based on Anne Moir and David Jessel's research; and Doreen Kimura, 'Sex differences in the brain', *Scientific American*, September 1992.

7 Quote from Anne Moir and David Jessel, *Brain Sex*, op. cit., p. 56.

8 Quote from Sally Helgesen, *The Female Advantage*, Doubleday Currency, New York, 1990, p. 37.

9 Herbert Landsell research noted in Anne Moir and David Jessel, *Brain Sex*, op. cit., p. 42.
10 Findings on the differences between female and male brains are still somewhat controversial. Research continues to be published in this area. At the time of writing this book, Anne Moir and David Jessel's *Brain Sex* and articles such as Doreen Kimura's 'Sex differences in the brain', published in *Scientific American*, September 1992, represent the most recent and readily accessible validations for our experiences and observations on gender differences in the context of the business world.
11 Quote from John Naisbitt and Patricia Aburdene, *Megatrends 2000*, William Morrow and Company, New York, 1990, p. 235.
12 The development of male and female brain structures is treated in detail in Anne Moir and David Jessel, *Brain Sex*, op. cit., chapter 2.
13 Quote from Anne Moir and David Jessel, *Brain Sex*, op. cit., p. 31.
14 John Gray has now written a book using a similar title, *Men are from Mars, Women are from Venus*, Thorsons, London, 1993, p. 31.
15 Quote from Robert Lawlor, *Earth Honouring*, Millennium Books, Australia, 1990, p. 48.

CHAPTER 5 GENDER TALK . . .

1 Michael Grinder, a US-based consultant and trainer, read a draft of this chapter and gave us some valuable input. Michael is a master trainer in the area of Neuro-Linguistic Programming (NLP) and he presents internationally recognised workshops for trainers, teachers and business people. (See note 10 for more information on NLP.)
2 Quote from Deborah Tannen, *You Just Don't Understand*, Random House, Sydney, 1991, p. 298.
3 The argument about 'genderlects' is developed and discussed by Deborah Tannen in her book, *You Just Don't Understand*, op. cit., chapter 1.
4 Quote on female speech habits from Marilyn Davidson, *Reach for the Top*, Judy Piatkus (Publishers), London, 1985, p. 82.
5 Perhaps it would be more accurate to say that adopting the male listening style may result in women being even more misunderstood by men than when they use their natural listening style. A male speaker tends to assume that a woman is agreeing with him when she is using her natural listening style, while a female speaker knows that what the other woman is doing is following the information. The information on listening styles is derived from Michael Grinder, *Listening Styles*.

6 Quote from Anita Roddick, *Body and Soul*, Ebury Press, London, 1991, pp. 17 and 21.

7 Deborah Tannen, *You Just Don't Understand*, op. cit., p. 297.

8 Adapted from ibid.

9 Carmel Niland, *Women, Power and the Political Process*, (unpublished) 1992.

10 John Grinder and Richard Bandler have developed a human science called Neuro-Linguistic Programming (NLP). Basically it is the study of words and how both verbal and non-verbal language affect our nervous system, which in turn affects our behaviour patterns, the actions we take and the results with which we end up.

11 Genie Z. Laborde, *Influencing with Integrity*, Syntony Publishing, California, 1987, pp. 28–9.

12 Mind mapping is explained in more detail in chapter 6.

13 Interview with Michael Grinder on 11 October 1992. Used with permission.

14 Michael Grinder, *Righting the Educational Conveyor Belt*, Metamorphous Press, Oregon, 1989, pp. 58–9.

15 Table adapted from Michael Grinder's diagram on neurological indicators in *Righting the Educational Conveyor Belt*, op. cit., p. 19.

16 Genie Laborde, *Influencing with Integrity*, op. cit., p. 56.

17 Michael Grinder made available US research which showed that K–8 (kindergarten to grade 8) schoolchildren had the following preferences:
   • visual: 42 per cent.
   • auditory: 22 per cent.
   • kinaesthetic: 37 per cent.

18 Definition of communication borrowed from the Powerful Presentations workshop, promoted by Excellerated Learning Institute.

19 See chapter 8 for some clues on developing new behaviours through role modelling.

20 Quote from interview with Michael Grinder on 11 October 1992. Used with permission.

21 Story from Philippa Bond, 28 April 1993. Used with permission. Philippa is a Sydney-based trainer and business consultant.

CHAPTER 6 DOING IT DIFFERENTLY . . .

1 The ideas developed in this chapter were incorporated into training and consulting sessions by two business consultants, Julie Wells and Celestine Michel. The final form of the chapter benefited greatly from their feedback.

2 Quote from Susan Jeffers, *Feel the Fear and Do it Anyway*, Arrow Books, London, 1987, p. 111.

3 Anthony Robbins, *Awaken the Giant Within*, Simon & Schuster, London, 1992, chapter 2.

4 Martin E. P. Seligman looks at optimism and pessimism in his book, *Learned Optimism*, Random House Australia, Sydney, 1990, p. 67.

5 The early work of Roger Sperry and Robert Ornstein is summarised by Tony Buzan in *Make the Most of Your Mind*, Pan Books, London, 1988, pp. 11–12.

6 Quote from Alvin Toffler, *Future Shock*, Pan Books, London, 1970, p. 361.

7 Warren Bennis, *On Becoming a Leader*, Century Business, London, 1990, p. 102.

8 Yin and yang are often described in the West as complementary polarities. Like night (yin) has its opposite, day (yang); female has male; anima has animus; negative has positive. One does not exist without the other—together they make up the whole. And when imbalance occcurs, as in the current patriarchal system, the laws of nature inevitably intervene to restore the balance.

9 Quote from Natasha Josefowitz, *Paths to Power*, Addison Wesley, Reading, Massachusetts, 1980, p. 148.

10 Hans Eysenck quoted in Edward de Bono, *Tactics*, Fontana Paperbacks, London, 1987, p. 158.

11 Brainstorming and synectics, among other creative techniques, are covered in many management textbooks.

12 Video, *Breakthrough: Beyond the Glass Ceiling*, Women & Management, Sydney, 1991.

13 More details on mind mapping can be found in Tony Buzan's *Make the Most of Your Mind*, op. cit., and an article by Bill Lee-Emery, 'Mind-mapping', in *Australian Wellbeing* magazine, No. 24, 1988.

14 From address by Jannie Tay to the National Conference on Women in Business and Management, Malaysia, 28 June 1993.

15 Interview with Celestine Michel on 13 August 1992. Used with permission.

16 Anita Roddick, *Body and Soul*, Ebury Press, London, 1991, pp. 176–8. Used with permission.

CHAPTER 7 CREATING YOUR FUTURE . . .

1 Blair Singer, of XCEL Training and Consulting, and two business

consultants, Wendy Buckingham and Patricia Gillard, read this chapter and offered some supportive feedback.

2 Quote from The Club of Rome, Making it Happen.

3 Quote from Mary Kay Ash. Source unknown.

4 John Kehoe, *Money, Success & You*, Zoetic Inc, Toronto, 1990, p. 44.

5 Research statistics cited in Anthony Robbins, *Unlimited Power*, Simon and Schuster, New York, 1986, p. 184.

6 Quote from Dudley Lynch & Paul L. Kordis, *Strategy of the Dolphin*, Arrow Books Limited, London, 1990, p. 163.

7 Interview with Carmel Niland on 26 September 1992. Used with permission.

8 Quote from Joel A. Barker from the video 'The Power of Vision', distributed by First Training, Australia, 1992.

9 Quote from Carmel Niland, 26 September 1992. Used with permission.

10 Quote from R. Buckminster Fuller, from the cassette tape series 'A week with Buckminster Fuller', recorded live, Kirkwood Meadows, Lake Tahoe, USA, 12–22 August 1981.

11 The information on precession is derived from R. Buckminster Fuller's book *Critical Path*, op. cit. In particular, refer to p. 141.

12 Genie Laborde, *Influencing with Integrity*, Syntony Publishing, California, 1987, pp. 146–7.

13 If you have difficulty with any of these steps, talk to a career consultant. A number of people are now specialising in this area, and many of them specialise in helping people in mid-life or contemplating career changes.

CHAPTER 8 FAST TRACKING TO SUCCESS . . .

1 Quote from John Naisbitt and Patricia Aburdene, *Megatrends 2000*, William Morrow and Company, New York, 1990, p. 240.

2 Quote from Anthony Robbins, *Unlimited Power*, Simon & Schuster, New York, 1986, p. 116.

3 Interview with Carolyn Brand on 15 June 1992. Used with permission.

4 Interview with Jannie Tay on 18 November 1992. Used with permission. Jannie Tay is the founder and managing director of The Hour Glass, a $200 million per annum business which has its head office in Singapore.

5 Interview with Meredith Hellicar on 2 November 1992. Used with

permission. At the time of the interview, Meredith Hellicar was the Executive Director of the New South Wales Coal Association.

6   Conscious role modelling sourced from Tad James and Wyatt Woodsmall, *Time Line Therapy and the Basis of Personality*, Meta Publications, California, US, 1988, pp. 40–1.

7   Quote from Warren Bennis, *On Becoming a Leader*, Century Business, London, 1990, p. 91.

8   Women of the World Mentoring can be contacted at PO Box 6645, Denver, Colorado 80206, USA.

9   Quote from Natasha Josefowitz, *Paths to Power*, Addison Wesley, Reading, Massachusetts, 1980, p. 99.

10 Quote from Jane White, *A Few Good Women: Breaking the Barriers to Top Management*, Prentice Hall, New Jersey, 1992, p. 71.

11 ibid., p. 123.

12 Quote from Gloria Steinem, *Outrageous Acts and Everyday Rebellions*, Holt Rinehart and Winston, New York, 1983.

13 Interview with Anita Roddick on 15 February 1993. Used with permission.

14 Leonie Still discusses the drawbacks of networking in her book, *Becoming a Top Woman Manager*, Allen & Unwin, Sydney, 1988, p. 85.

15 Laura Hwang, 'Women in business—changing trends, *Business Times*, Singapore, 9 July 1992.

16 Interview with D. C. Cordova on 15 August 1992. Used with permission. D. C. was one of two female business partners of Robert Kiyosaki. Between them they ran the Excellerated Learning Institute until 1994. Refer to chapter 1, note 10.

17 Article on Mary Robinson, President of Ireland, by Greg Sheridan in the *Weekend Australian*, 24–5 October 1992, p. 21.

18 Interview with Patricia Forsythe on 2 September 1992. Used with permission.

CHAPTER 9 BEYOND THE COMFORT ZONE . . .

1   Quote from Susan Jeffers, *Feel the Fear and Do it Anyway*, Arrow Books, London, 1987, p. 118.

2   Interview with Anne Fairbairn, Australian poet and artist, on 28 September 1992. Used with permission.

3   Robert Kiyosaki in his book, *If You Want to Be Rich and Happy . . . don't go to school*, Excellerated Learning Publishing, California, 1991,

offers some powerful thoughts about the ineffectiveness of the Western education system.

4 Quote from Natasha Josefowitz, *Paths to Power*, Addison Wesley, Reading, Massachusetts, 1980, p. 59.

5 Article on Anita Roddick by Richard Keeves 'Anita Roddick, the Enlightened Capitalist', in *Business Directions*, Issue 34, 1992, pp. 23–5.

6 Susan Jeffers, *Feel the Fear and Do it Anyway*, op. cit., p. 124.

7 Quote from Dudley Lynch & Paul L. Kordis, *Strategy of the Dolphin*, Arrow Books Limited, London, 1990, pp. 153–4.

8 Interview with Anne Fairbairn, Australian poet and artist, on 28 September 1992. Used with permission.

9 Kate Lyons, 'Women in Bu$iness', *Australian Small Business and Investing*, July 1992.

CHAPTER 10 WALKING THE TALK . . .

1 Quote from John Naisbitt and Patricia Aburdene, *Megatrends 2000*, William Morrow and Company, New York, 1990, p. 240.

2 Quote from Warren Bennis, *On Becoming a Leader*, Century Business, London, 1990, p. 5.

3 ibid., pp. 5 and 39–42.

4 Interview with Meredith Hellicar on 2 November 1992. Used with permission.

5 The importance of leadership at all levels is stressed by John Humphrey, 'A time of 10,000 leaders', *Executive Excellence*, June 1991, p. 17 and Charles Handy, *The Age of Unreason*, Arrow Books, London, 1989, chapters 5 and 6.

6 Quote from Professor Leonie Still in the video 'Breakthrough: Beyond the Glass Ceiling', Women & Management Inc., Sydney, 1991.

7 Definition from *The Concise Oxford Dictionary*, Sixth Edition, Oxford University Press, Oxford, 1976.

8 Interview with Michael Grinder on 11 October 1992. Used with permission.

9 Quote from Alvin Toffler, *Powershift*, Bantam Books, New York, 1991, p. 20.

10 Quote from Judith Vogt and Kenneth Murrell, *Empowerment in Organisations*, University Associates Inc., California, 1990, p. 29.

11 Statistics from Natasha Josefowitz, *Paths to Power*, Addison Wesley, Reading, Massachusetts, 1980, p. 195; *Half Way to Equal*, Report of

the Inquiry into Equal Opportunity and Equal Status for Women in Australia, Australian Government Publishing Service, Canberra, 1992, pp. 51 and 165; John Naisbitt and Patricia Aburdene, *Megatrends 2000*, William Morrow and Company, New York, 1990, pp. 217 and 226; Australian Bureau of Statistics, *Labour Force Australia Study*, February 1992; Kate Lyons, 'Women In Bu$iness', *Australian Small Business and Investing*, July 1992; *Sunday Times*, London, 14 February 1993; *Asian Business*, November 1993; 'Boards of Directors in Australia', Korn/Ferry International, Australian Institute of Company Directors, Thirteenth Study, 1994.

12 Paraphrased from John Naisbitt and Patricia Aburdene, *Megatrends 2000*, op. cit., p. 235.

13 Interview with Carolyn Brand on 15 June 1992. Used with permission.

14 Quote from Alvin Toffler, *Powershift*, Bantam Books, New York, 1991, p. 195.

15 Quote from Sally Helgesen, *The Female Advantage*, Doubleday Currency, New York, 1990, p. 39.

16 ibid., chapter 1.

17 On the less positive side, by seeing their jobs as just one part of their whole identity, it is more costly for women to fail as they tend to feel it more personally than men (TV series, 'Brain Sex', Primedia Productions Limited, 1993, episode 2).

18 Interview with Anita Roddick on 15 February 1993. Used with permission.

19 Articles on Jannie Tay in the *Productivity Digest*, Singapore, November 1991 and the *Straits Times*, 1 November 1991.

20 Article on Jannie Tay in the *Straits Times*, 1 November 1991.

21 Quote by Mary Robinson at a conference on women and leadership in Dublin in July 1992, taken from 'Not a Bedroom War', SBS-TV, Anne Deveson Productions, Sydney, 1993.

22 Quote from Natasha Josefowitz, *Paths to Power*, op. cit., p. 194.

23 Interview with Grace M. Atkinson on 8 December 1992. Used with permission.

24 Rensis Likert in 'The principle of supportive relationships' in D. S. Pugh (ed.), *Organization Theory*, Penguin Books, London, 1976, pp. 289–92, describes traditional organisation structures.

25 Sally Helgesen develops the concept of the web structure in *The Female Advantage*, op. cit.

26 The word 'courage' comes from the French word *coeur*, which means heart.

27 Quote by Mary Robinson in 'Not a Bedroom War', op. cit.

CHAPTER 11 BRIGHTNESS FOR THE FUTURE!!

1 Quote from R. L. Wing (ed.), *The Tao of Power*, Aquarian/Thorsons, London, 1986, Number 28.

2 David Suzuki, *Time to Change*, Allen & Unwin, Sydney, 1993, pp. 190, 192.

3 Article by Adrian McGregor in the *Sydney Morning Herald*, 20 March 1993.

4 Quote from Patricia Aburdene and John Naisbitt, *Megatrends For Women*, Villard Books, New York, 1992, p. 324.

5 Article on Mary Robinson by Greg Sheridan in the *Weekend Australian*, 24–25 October 1992, p. 21.

6 Judith Warner, *Hillary Clinton—The Inside Story*, Penguin Group, New York, 1993, p. 234.

7 ibid., p. 243.

8 Anita Roddick, *Body and Soul*, Ebury Press, London, 1991, p. 77.

9 ibid., p. 235.

10 ibid., p. 235.

11 Robert Kiyosaki, *If You Want to be Rich and Happy . . . don't go to school*, Excellerated Learning Publishing, California, 1991, pp. 99–100.

12 Article in *Eve*, Singapore, November 1992.

13 Interview with Meredith Hellicar on 2 November 1992. Used with permission.

14 For the unusual perspective on the childrearing habits of the royal family we wish to acknowledge Carmel Niland, Director, Carmel Niland & Associates, a Sydney-based consulting firm.

15 The electronic village is discussed in Charles Handy, *The Age of Unreason*, Arrow Books, London, 1989, pp. 84–7 and Joel A. Barker, *Discovering the Future: the Business of Paradigms*, I. L. I. Press, St Paul, Minnesota, 1989, p. 103.

16 Our discussions with Carmel Niland on 26 September 1992 helped in developing parts of the section 'Playing outside the box'.

17 For the ideas on women as pioneers we wish to acknowledge Dave Ulrich in his article 'Competing from the inside out', *Executive Excellence*, June 1991.

18 Naomi Wolf, *Fire with Fire*, Chatto & Windus, London, 1993, p. xvi.

19 Quote from R. Buckminster Fuller, *Cosmography*, Macmillan Publishing Company, New York, 1992, pp. 48 and 57.

EXERCISES

1 Exercise on values partially sourced from Tad James and Wyatt Woodsmall, *Time Line Therapy and the Basis of Personality*, op. cit. chapters 21 and 22.

2 'How to' exercise based on information from Tad James and Wyatt Woodsmall, *Time Line Therapy and the Basis of Personality*, chapters 21 and 22.

3 For more details on sensory systems (visual, auditory, kinaesthetic) see chapter 5.

4 Other examples of how to change, delete and add new values are contained in books recommended in the bibliography.

5 Questionnaire sourced from Patricia Scallon, Walter B. Barbe, Michael N. Milone, Jr and Michael Grinder; University Associates.

6 Original source of brain dominance questionnaire unknown. It has been adapted and used by Robin Lovell and Sofie Ghersetti, SEEK Seminars, Australia.

REFERENCES AND RECOMMENDED READING

Abdoolcarim, Zoher 'How women are winning at work', *Asian Business,* November 1993, pp. 24–29

Aburdene, Patricia and Naisbitt, John *Megatrends for Women,* Villard Books, New York, 1992

Bandler, Richard *Using Your Brain for a Change,* Real People Press, Utah, 1985

Bardwick, Judith M. *Danger in the Comfort Zone,* AMACOM, New York, 1991

Barker, Joel A. *Discovering the Future: the Business Of Paradigms,* I. L. I. Press, St Paul, Minnesota, 1989

Bennis, Warren *On Becoming a Leader,* Century Business, London, 1990

de Bono, Edward *de Bono's Thinking Course,* BBC, London, 1982

——, *Tactics,* Fontana Paperbacks, London, 1987

Buzan, Tony *Make the Most of Your Mind,* Pan Books, London, 1988

Chater, Kerry and Gaster, Roma (eds) *Breakthrough: Beyond the Glass Ceiling Trainers Guide,* Women & Management Inc., Sydney, Australia, 1992

Cohen, Sherry Suib *Tender Power,* Addison Wesley Publishing Co. Inc., US, 1989

Covey, Stephen R. *Principle-centered Leadership,* Simon & Schuster, London, 1992

Davidson, Marilyn *Reach for the Top,* Judy Piatkus (Publishers), London, 1985

de Beauvoir, Simone *The Second Sex,* Penguin Books, England, 1975

Drucker, Peter F. *Managing for the Future,* Butterworth-Heinemann Ltd, London, 1992

Faludi, Susan *Backlash: The Undeclared War Against Women,* Chatto & Windus, London, 1992

French, Marilyn *The War against Women*, Hamish Hamilton, London, 1992

Fuller, R. Buckminster *Cosmography*, Macmillan Publishing Company, New York, 1992

——, *Critical Path*, St Martin's Press, New York, 1981

——, *Operating Manual for Spaceship Earth*, NAL Penguin Inc., New York, 1971

Gleick, James *Chaos*, Cardinal Books, London, 1989

Grinder, Michael *Righting the Educational Conveyor Belt*, Metamorphous Press, Oregon, 1989

Half Way to Equal, Report of the Inquiry into Equal Opportunity and Equal Status for Women in Australia, Australian Government Publishing Service, Canberra, 1992

Handy, Charles *The Age of Unreason*, Arrow Books, London, 1989

Heider, John *The Tao of Leadership*, Bantam Books, New York, 1988

Helgesen, Sally *The Female Advantage*, Doubleday Currency, New York, 1990

Humphrey, John 'A time of 10,000 leaders', *Executive Excellence*, June 1991

James, Tad *Creating Your Future*, ProfitAbility Group, Inc., Hawaii, 1989

James, Tad and Woodsmall, Wyatt *Time Line Therapy and the Basis of Personality*, Meta Publications, California, US, 1988

Jeffers, Susan *Feel the Fear and Do it Anyway*, Arrow Books, London, 1987

Josefowitz, Natasha *Paths to Power*, Addison Wesley, Reading, Massachusetts, 1980

Kehoe, John *Money Success and You*, Zoetic Inc., Toronto, 1990

Kiyosaki, Robert *If You Want to Be Rich and Happy . . . Don't Go to School*, Excellerated Learning Publishing, California, 1991

LaBella, Arleen and Leach, Dolores *Personal Power*, New View Press, Colorado, 1983

Laborde, Genie Z. *Fine Tune Your Brain*, Syntony Publishing, California, 1988

——, *Influencing with Integrity*, Syntony Publishing, California, 1987

Lawlor, Robert *Earth Honouring*, Millennium Books, Sydney, 1990

Lynch, Dudley and Kordis, Paul L. *Strategy of the Dolphin*, Arrow Books Limited, London, 1990

Mackay, Hugh *Reinventing Australia*, Angus & Robertson, Sydney, 1993

Meares, Ainslie *The Hidden Powers of Leadership*, Hill of Content Publishing, Melbourne, 1978

Miles, Rosalind *The Women's History of the World*, Paladin, London 1989

Mitchell, Susan *The Matriarchs*, Penguin Books Australia Ltd, Melbourne, 1987

——, *Tall Poppies*, Penguin Books Australia Ltd, Melbourne, 1984

——, *Tall Poppies Too*, Penguin Books Australia Ltd, Melbourne, 1991

Moir, Anne and Jessel, David *Brain Sex*, Mandarin Paperback, London, 1989

Myers, Isabel Briggs *Gifts Differing*, Consulting Psychologists Press, Palo Alto, 1980

Naisbitt, John and Aburdene, Patricia *Megatrends 2000*, William Morrow and Company, New York, 1990

Neave, Henry R. *The Deming Dimension*, SPC Press Inc., Tennessee, 1990

O'Connor, Joseph and Seymour, John *Introducing Neuro-Linguistic Programming*, Mandala, UK, 1990

Ohmae, Kenichi *The Borderless World*, Fontana, London, 1991

Peters, Tom *Thriving on Chaos*, Macmillan, London, 1988

Peters, Tom J. and Robert. H. Waterman Jr, *In Search of Excellence*, Harper & Row, New York, 1982

Pugh, D. S. (ed.) *Organization Theory*, Penguin Books, London, 1976

Reed, Evelyn *Woman's Evolution—from Matriarchal Clan to Patriarchal Family*, Pathfinder Press, New York, 1975

Robbins, Anthony *Awaken the Giant Within*, Simon and Schuster, London, 1992

——, *Unlimited Power*, Simon and Schuster, New York, 1988

Roddick, Anita *Body and Soul*, Ebury Press, London, 1991

Seligman, Martin E. P. *Learned Optimism*, Random House Australia, Sydney, 1990

Smith, Neville and Ainsworth, Murray *Ideas Unlimited*, Nelson Publishers, Melbourne, 1985

Steinem, Gloria *Outrageous Acts and Everyday Rebellions*, Holt Rinehart and Winston, New York, 1983

——, *Revolution from Within: a Book of Self-esteem*, Bloomsbury Publishing Ltd, London, 1992

Still, Leonie *Becoming a Top Woman Manager*, Allen & Unwin, Sydney, 1988

——, *Everything a Woman Needs to Know about Winning the Corporate Battle*, Horwitz Grahame, Sydney, 1986

Summers, Anne *Damned Whores and God's Police*, Penguin Books Ltd, Melbourne, 1975

Suzuki, David *Time to Change*, Allen & Unwin, Sydney, 1993

Tannen, Deborah *You Just Don't Understand*, Random House, Sydney, 1991

Toffler, Alvin *Powershift*, Bantam Books, New York, 1991

Vogt, Judith and Murrell, Kenneth *Empowerment in Organisations*, University Associates Inc., California, 1990

Warner, Judith *Hillary Clinton—the Inside Story*, Penguin Group, New York, 1993

White, Jane *A Few Good Women: Breaking the Barriers to Top Management*, Prentice Hall, New Jersey, 1992

Wing, R. L. (ed.) *The Tao of Power*, Aquarian/Thorsons, London, 1986

Wolf, Naomi *The Beauty Myth*, Vintage, London, 1990

——, *Fire with Fire*, Chatto & Windus, London, 1993

INDEX

HEART
of business

Heart of Business is an organisation, founded by Kerry Chater and Roma Gaster, that is dedicated to a new philosophy of business—a philosophy that focuses on caring, trust, empowerment and valuing differences, that believes in looking at the global perspective, in joint venturing, in sharing information and working with others, in continuous learning, and in supporting women and men who are willing to embrace this new philosophy for the good of all humanity, wildlife and the environment.

Please contact us if you would like further information on any of the following:

- The cassette series, 'The Equality Myth'
- Audio cassettes and workshops on
    - recognising and valuing gender and cultural diversity
    - helping women realise their potential
    - new directions in leadership
    - changing organisation structures
    - developing a global business ethic

Heart of Business
PO Box 83
Bondi Beach NSW 2026
Australia
Phone: (61 2) 365 4470 or (61 2) 398 5170
Fax: (61 2) 365 2477